Life after Loss

FOURTH EDITION

LIFE

after

LOSS

A Practical Guide to Renewing Your
Life after Experiencing Major Loss

BOB DEITS

Da Capo

LIFE
LONG

A Member of the
Perseus Books Group

Set in 11.5 point Goudy by the Perseus Books Group

Cataloging-in-Publication data for this book is available from the Library of Congress.

Lifelong Books edition 2004

Library of Congress Cataloging-in-Publication Data

Deits, Bob, 1933-
    Life after loss : a practical guide to renewing your life after experiencing major loss / B ob Deits.—4th ed.
        p. cm.
    Includes bibliographical references and index.
    ISBN-13 978-0-306-81314-6 (pbk. : alk. paper)
    ISBN-10 0-306-81314-9 (pbk. : alk. paper)
    1. Loss (Psychology) 2. Life change events—Psychological aspects. 3. Bereavement—Psychological aspects. 4. Grief. I. Title.
    BF575.D35D45 2004
    155.9'3—dc22

                                                                    2003028222

Published by Lifelong Books
A Member of the Perseus Books Group
http://www.dacapopress.com

Lifelong books are available at special discounts for bulk purchases in the U.S. by corporations, institutions, and other organizations. For more information, please contact the Special Markets Department at the Perseus Books Group, 11 Cambridge Center, Cambridge, MA 02142, or call (800) 255–1514 or (617) 252-5298, or e-mail special.markets@perseusbooks.com.

    8 9 10 11 12 13 14 15—10 09 08 07 06

This books is dedicated to . . .

Those courageous people who shared
their lives and losses with me through grief support groups.

Dr. Howard Clinebell Jr., who taught me the
deeper meanings of pastoral care.

Dr. Earl Grollman, a compassionate
genius in healing losses.

June Deits, who has shared life with me
"for better or for worse" since we were eighteen years old.

CONTENTS

INTRODUCTION

It has been more than fifteen years since the first edition of *Life after Loss* was published. I never dreamed there would be multiple editions in several languages to follow, or that it would become "One of the classics in the field of crisis intervention," as Dr. Earl Grollman noted when the third edition came out in 2000.

Year after year, I have continued to be immersed in the major losses people experience—and the grief those losses inevitably produce. The second and third editions reflected my growth in understanding the nature of major losses and the importance of learning to grieve effectively. During those years, my family and I had our own losses. Those personal experiences also informed the content of *Life after Loss*. Each new edition has brought new insights and resources for coping with the greatest challenges life brings us.

Now, it's time to expand the scope of the book again.

The events of September 11, 2001, represented a terrible loss to people in the United States and around the world. The horror of that day resulted in a sense of grief on a national scale that has exceeded anything in the history of this country. The economic impact worldwide will be felt for decades.

People have a difficult time putting their feelings into words. There is a sense of being violated in a way no one thought was possible. Anger, frustration, and insecurity have merged into one pervasive emotion: *fear*. That fear only grew with the invasion of Iraq. The images of war were before the world in living and dying color twenty-four hours a day.

With the fear has come a loss of freedom. Airline travel is down here and abroad, warnings of further terrorist attacks are coded by color to indicate the level of threat, and we have learned a new vocabulary that

x   Life after Loss

contains such words as "anthrax" and "small pox" and "weapons of mass destruction."

We need to find new ways to live with freedom and without fear. Just as we must overcome personal losses to have a full life, we must overcome the fear to find the freedom. The challenge is the same: How do we establish equilibrium again? How do we have less tears and more laughter?

A good starting place is to remember that of all the dangers in life, an act of terrorism is one of the least likely to happen. We are a million times more likely to die in an accident at home than we are at the hands of any terrorist. In response to the terror of being a Jew in a Nazi death camp, famed psychologist Viktor Frankl later wrote: "Everything can be taken from a man but . . . the last of the human freedoms—to choose one's attitude in any given set of circumstances, to choose one's own way."[1] Making choices about your response to any loss, personal or national, is still one of your greatest assets.

As it was with the previous editions, this book is as much for *doing* as it is for reading. It addresses the full scope of major losses we experience just because we are real people living in a real world. It offers practical, useful, and well-proven ways not only to make it through any loss but also to come out on top feeling like a winner.

> This book is as much for *doing* as it is for reading.

You will find another new chapter titled "Losses in Later Life." We are a population that is getting older. Soon, the first of the Baby Boomers, those born between 1946 and 1964, will begin turning sixty. I have to tell you that getting older sneaks up on you. When the first edition of *Life after Loss* was published, I couldn't even spell "senior citizen"—and now, as the story goes, "I are one."

It's a different time of life, and it brings new and challenging experiences. The golden years are not without tarnish. It's another of those events for which we are not prepared—but we can and we should be prepared. You will find insights that will help you help the older people in your life and that will make you ready for your own journey into your later years.

There is an entire category of losses that can be gathered under the heading "Quiet Losses." They would include being sexually abused as a child or adult or such things as women losing breasts and men losing sexual potency because of cancer surgeries. The pain of these losses can be as intense as the death of a loved one. However, it is often much more difficult to talk about them and thus to find comfort and healing.

There is a special chapter in this book devoted to such quiet losses. For some readers, this will be the most important chapter in the book. My wife, June, has shared in writing this part of the book. She speaks as a survivor of both childhood sexual abuse and of breast cancer that resulted in a mastectomy. Her courage to break the silence around these quiet losses has brought hope and new life to all who have heard her speak at seminars and workshops. Now, she shares her insights with you in this special chapter.

The subject of God and the role of religion in coping with our losses are always sensitive issues. In spite of all the scientific information to the contrary, we still have a strong temptation to embrace "Make-a-Wish" religion. That might be okay if it didn't create so much unnecessary additional heartbreak when a major loss occurs. Your religious beliefs can be a tremendous resource for grief recovery—or an almost insurmountable barrier to healing. You will find practical help with the spiritual dimension of grief as with every other aspect of the experience.

Even if you have not yet experienced a major loss, you know someone who has. The question we all ask at such a time is, "What can I do to help?" This book is as useful as a caregiver's manual for helping as it is for those who have had the loss. Not only can you give it as a gift that will make a difference for years to come, by reading it yourself you will know what to say and what not to say, what to do—and not do—to be helpful.

The ultimate purpose of this book, whatever the loss might be, is the survival of the survivors. Researchers have known for many years that we face increased risks for cancer, heart disease, diabetes, and other chronic illnesses after a major loss. It was Dr. Glen Davidson and his team at Southern Illinois University who identified the factors of this increased risk. They also spelled out how to avoid that risk. The results of their work have been incorporated into the *doing* part of this book.

When you have finished reading, you will know how to cope with the greatest challenges life can bring. You will know the difference between normal grief and grief that is distorted. You will be aware of warning signs that indicate it is time to seek professional intervention. You will learn how to take care of yourself physically while your emotions are being healed.

Exercises and suggestions to help you recover your happiness and protect your health are spelled out in detail throughout this book. They have worked for thousands of others, and they can work for you, too.

You can take charge of your own journey through grief just as others have done by following the steps given in the pages that follow. The largest of losses is not the end of life for you.

Believe it or not, the act of grieving can be an avenue for personal growth. You will experience the truth of this through the real-life stories of people who have faced the worst and have come out on top.

> You can have a satisfying, contented, and meaningful life after any loss.

The first three editions of *Life after Loss* have helped more than one hundred thousand people learn the skills of effective grief work. This new fourth edition can make it possible for you to join their ranks.

1

Loss and the Mourning After

The one universal human experience

The one common human experience is losing someone or something near and dear to us. These major losses happen to everyone without regard to economic status, ethnic origin, religious belief, or gender. If there is any good news, it is that we are never the only one to feel as we do.

The emotional pain is beyond words. Therefore, no response is more normal or appropriate than grief.

Major loss and the grief that follows remain among the most misunderstood of all human experiences. When a friend loses a loved one to death, we don't know what to say. The same is true if that person goes through a divorce, is diagnosed with cancer, or has a business that fails.

It's worse when the loss happens to you. You don't have words to express what you are feeling. The pain can exceed the worst toothache you ever had. Some friends and family members will pull back, leaving you feeling abandoned. It may seem as if you have fallen into a pit from which there is no escape. The world around you will act as if you should be back on your feet and functioning as though nothing had happened in a matter of days—a couple of weeks at the most. You can't do it— and you shouldn't.

You need to hear this: *Experiencing a terrible loss and the grief that goes with it is the most concrete proof there is that you are a normal, real, live human being.*

The first goal of this book is to help keep you from making the worst experience of your life worse than it already is. It's bad enough all by itself.

You will make it worse by

- Having unreasonable expectations of yourself.
- Keeping your feelings and thoughts inside instead of talking about them with understanding people.
- Believing that your religious faith can lessen the impact of your loss.
- Assuming that you are the only one who has ever had such sadness.
- Thinking you will always feel as you do in the first weeks.

You can also make the task more difficult by not taking your loss as seriously as you could.

You expect to grieve when a friend or loved one dies. But it is equally important to mourn the death of a relationship, a divorce, the loss of familiar surroundings when relocating to another city, the loss of a job, or any other loss that makes a major impact on the quality of your happiness. All the risk factors that follow a death also apply to other major losses.

If you even suspect that you may have been the victim of sexual abuse as a child, you are among a large group of people who have experienced this horrible trauma. Statistics indicate that more women than men have faced this "loss of innocence," but the pain is just as great and the grief process just as difficult, regardless of gender.

Losing a body part to surgery is often more painful emotionally than physically. Women who have mastectomies in order to survive breast cancer often struggle as much with the loss of their breasts as they do with having the disease. The same is true for men who have prostate surgery and have their sexual function damaged. These kinds of procedures can leave emotional scars that are far deeper than those on the body.

The death of a pet can be a terribly difficult experience for many people.

Throughout this book, you will find guidance on how to avoid or overcome making your journey through grief worse than it has to be.

The Universal Experience

Loss is a fact of being alive in our world, and no one is immune from the experience. Rabbi Harold Kushner was absolutely correct—bad things do happen to good people.

Major loss affects good people, the not-so-good people, and everyone in between. It does not check out the color of your skin or your ethnic origin or see if you are a faithful giver to your church or synagogue.

One of the more challenging facts of loss is that having one major loss does not prevent you from having other losses. You need this book because *Life after Loss* will help you cope with present and future losses. Consider this:

- We live in a mortal, frail, imperfect world in which the word *fair* doesn't always apply.
- Every marriage ends one of two ways: death or divorce.
- Life is always a terminal condition.
- Every career has an end.
- Every relationship is temporary.
- The aging process is inevitable and so are the increased losses that come with it.

> We live in a mortal, frail, imperfect world in which the word *fair* doesn't always apply.

Now for Some Good News

You can get through every major loss without being destroyed by it. You can enjoy life to the fullest, knowing all the while that it has an end point. Everybody is capable of becoming effective at doing grief work.

Healthy grief is not a passive experience. It isn't something that happens to you. The loss is what happens to you—grief is the normal, appropriate response to loss. Grieving is something you do to heal the wounds in your life after a major loss. There is much more for you to do in response to any loss than just wait and suffer. You can actually take charge of your own grief process. You are the one person who can turn the pain of any loss into a creative hurt—an experience from which you learn and grow.

The exercises you will find in subsequent chapters will teach you how to do everything from getting a good night's sleep to being able to enjoy eating again to learning how to cry.

Real Stories of Real People's Victories

Matthew was diagnosed with cancer on the day of his fourteenth wedding anniversary. His wife, Barbara, was at his side through chemotherapy. He seemed fine for awhile, except for an unrelated back problem that resulted in surgery. The pain persisted even after the surgery. More tests revealed more cancer. Again, treatment seemed to be effective, but he grew steadily weaker. He had trouble breathing and tired quickly. This time, the tests revealed not cancer but pulmonary fibrosis—a side effect of the chemotherapy.

Four years after his cancer was diagnosed, Matthew died of pulmonary fibrosis.

Barbara was heartbroken and angry. She questioned why doctors could save him from cancer but killed him with the treatment. She was angry with God, who she felt had deserted them.

When Barbara came to our grief support group, she didn't have much to say that was positive. Efforts to reach out to her were often met with sarcastic rejection. However, she kept coming, and over the course of time, a new person began to emerge.

Barbara would tell you that the key was the day she was able to forgive herself for not being able to save Matthew.

Today, she is a positive, outgoing person who is the life of any party she attends. She drives a large motor home across country by herself and maintains a family cabin in the mountains. She sings in the church's choir, ushers, and serves as a volunteer care-giver to elderly people.

The life Barbara has is not the one she would have chosen for herself. Given a choice, she would give up anything to have Matthew back again. But she has a full, rewarding life that is good in its own way. She is also a stronger person for having overcome the tragedy life gave her.

Jan's story is different, but the pain was just as great. Jan was an accomplished roller skate dancer. She was as graceful on skates as she was dedicated to her sport.

That all changed just before Christmas one year. Jan was on her way to go caroling with her church group. A man ran a red light and broadsided her car. She was not wearing a seat belt. The impact threw her across the seat, and her head hit the passenger side door.

It was several weeks before she woke up out of her coma. When she did, it was clear that she had sustained serious and permanent damage to the motor section of her brain.

She had to learn to read and write—and to walk—again. Her sense of balance has been damaged so that skating is not possible. The amnesia she has from the trauma has blocked out any memory of skating.

Jan walks every day. She has again joined a choir. She goes to the skating rink and takes photos of the other skaters, then gives them the pictures. Jan also spends time online and is a source of funny stories and poignant anecdotes to a large group of friends.

She talks freely about the parts of her experience she can remember. She is not bitter about the challenges she faces. Jan is another one who has found a good and meaningful life after a terrible loss.

Both Jan and Barbara went through a time of grief that was normal and healthy. The feelings they experienced were appropriate to the magnitude of their losses.

The grief recovery both of them have achieved is not like getting over a case of the flu or any other illness. It's like getting knocked flat on your back and working to recover equilibrium in your life.

It's this kind of grief recovery that you can have as well.

It Takes Time

Because it is an appropriate response to loss, grief is not a bad word! Neither is it a sign of weakness, nor does it represent a lack of religious faith. Grief isn't something to avoid at all costs and "get over" as quickly as possible. It isn't better to feel joy than to feel grief. It is certainly *more fun* to feel joy—but it isn't better. If something good is happening, it is appropriate to be joyful. If you have experienced loss, it is equally appropriate to be sad.

One of the greatest experiences of my life was standing in the delivery room of a hospital and watching our daughter give birth to her daughter on my birthday. It was an incredible gift of love and trust that our daughter invited not only her mother but also me to be present. That it happened on my birthday made it a rare experience indeed. If I was not overjoyed beyond words in that setting, I would be crazy by definition. In the same way, when my six-year-old brother-in-law was killed, I would have been crazy by definition if I wasn't buried under unspeakable sorrow.

The key word is *appropriate*.

If you have had a major loss, you already know that well-meaning friends will reward you if you can keep from crying in public. You will be told how strong you are and how "well" you are doing.

The problem is, *not* crying is an inappropriate behavior that can put you at great risk of physical and emotional illness. Anyone who wants you to hold your grief in check is seeking their own comfort—not yours. To heal properly, you must express your sadness freely and for as long as it takes to release it.

Many polls and studies have asked the public, "How long should it take to mourn the death of a loved one?" The most common answer is "between forty-eight hours and two weeks." In truth, we have barely started grieving in that length of time. Research by Dr. Glen Davidson, a pioneer in analyzing the bereavement process, revealed it takes most people at least two years to begin returning to a normal life after a major loss.

There is even danger in establishing two years as a reasonable goal. I have known people who took as long as five years to finish mourning and came out healthy and strong. Yogi Berra, the colorful former major league baseball player and manager, once said that a baseball game isn't over until its over. That's the way it is with the grief process. It's finished when it's finished.

I frequently hear a bereaved person say, "I'm so relieved to know that others still don't have everything worked out. I thought I was the only one who wasn't handling my loss as I should."

Very little is reasonable about grief. There is nothing sensible, reasonable, or fair about losing someone we love. Nothing is easy about having a marriage end in divorce. Actually, there is nothing rational about *any* major loss. Whatever the loss, the experience is devastating. The last thing any of us needs at such a time is to feel guilty because we aren't responding in the "right" way.

If you are having problems with a loss after two, three, or four years, it only means you aren't finished with your grief. It doesn't make you weak. It doesn't make you less of a person. It just means you still have work to do. You don't have to feel embarrassed or shy about seeking help in doing it. My dad used to say there are those who enjoy hitting their thumbs with a hammer because it feels so good when they quit. Don't inflict additional and unnecessary pain on yourself when you are grieving.

If you are surprised by the true length of the grieving process, you aren't alone. It isn't negative or morbid. A grief reaction means the loss was significant and life-changing for you. The sadness and emptiness you feel are appropriate. It helps to remember this: ***Grief is the last act of love we have to give those who have died.***

Grief is the final way we can say, "I care about you, and you matter to me very much."

Dr. Earl Grollman, internationally known counselor on death and bereavement, has said that the loss of a loved is the most stressful of all life's

> Grief is the last act of love we have to give those who have died.

changes: "You may look into the mirror and not even recognize the way you now look. Something in you is gone that can never be regained."

Your grief is a symbol of the quality of relationship you had with one who has died. Rather than trying to hide your grief, I encourage you to wear the signs of it as a badge of honor. Your tears, the heaviness in your heart, and the overwhelming sense of loneliness all say, "This person, this marriage, this part of my life has been so important to me that nothing will ever be the same again. My grief is the last act of love I have to give, and I will wear it with pride."

Other Kinds of Loss

Not everything is bad in a marriage that ends in divorce. The worst of marriages has seen shared times that are good and meaningful. These, too, are worthy of your grief.

The fact of divorce can be a terrible loss in itself. Nancy said to me, "I think I grieved over the fact that I was now a divorcée. It was a label I never wanted."

There is nothing wrong with acknowledging the significance of our attachment to a familiar place by grieving the loss of that place when we move away. Even less significant losses in your life will hang around in the recesses of your memory and emotions, gathering energy until they have enough combined force to make themselves felt.

Grief and Accumulated Loss

Have you ever found yourself overreacting to a minor disappointment? Do you have times when you are irritable and short-tempered without knowing why? Such behavior often results when some relatively minor loss experience calls forth the gathered energy of several buried losses from the past—losses that were not adequately acknowledged at the time they occurred. Thinking back about these losses is not enjoyable, but it is necessary if they are to be healed.

The desert community in which we live often experiences a gathering of thunderhead clouds on summer afternoons. Sometimes the result is little more than higher humidity and soft breezes. On other occasions the breezes become a screaming dust storm, followed by intense rain. These monsoons happen when the atmosphere has stored up the right conditions and something serves as the trigger to turn it loose.

Our accumulation of loss experiences is like that. We store them up over time until something happens to trigger the outpouring of all our pent-up feelings. It should be no surprise that we sometimes cry our eyes out over a seemingly minor disappointment.

Norman Cousins said, "Death is not the enemy. Living in constant fear of it is." I would paraphrase that to say, "*Loss* is not the enemy. Living in constant fear of it is."

Because of books such as this one, the lid is off the subject of loss and grief. Earl Grollman once noted that "Grief is the last pornography." I don't think that is the case any longer. It is no longer taboo to say you are grieving. As we begin accepting grief as an appropriate and normal response to loss, it becomes something we are free to experience without seeing ourselves as weak. Understanding it isn't a forbidden subject; we can lay aside any sense of guilt and break the silence about our experience. We can take the opportunity to grieve at the time the loss occurs—and for as long as it takes to recover from it.

These are the first steps toward discovering a full and rewarding life after any loss.

2

First Responses to a Major Loss

When the bad news comes

Years ago, I attended a conference and was sitting in an auditorium with about five hundred other people. Messages were posted for participants on a large chalkboard at the front. I saw a messenger go to the board but paid little attention until I saw him write down my own name. I had an urgent call. When I reached the telephone, someone told me my mother was dead. To this day I can't remember who broke the bad news.

Mom was only fifty-four years old. Although I knew her history of health problems, I never suspected she would die so young. She had just begun a new treatment and was responding well. No one considered her illness life-threatening. While I was at the conference, she died in her sleep.

I turned from the telephone in that state of hazy confusion I have seen so often in others after a major loss. I didn't know what to do next. At that moment our minister appeared and I muttered in a flat voice, "My mother died."

Responding to Death

What happens when you are told a loved one is dead? Most of us go into a state of shock and are apt to do just about anything. The first seven days are often a blur about which little is remembered later.

It's nearly impossible to do much in the first few hours and days after news of a loss. You can't anticipate how you will react to the death of someone dear to you. Even if you have had other losses before, each experience is different and you may react in quite different ways.

Whatever your reaction is to the bad news, it will be normal and okay. Some people faint; others are icy calm. Some fall apart in tears, while others become the world's greatest organizers. No particular reaction is better or worse than any other. It doesn't mean you cared less if you don't become hysterical. You aren't weak if you cry or courageous if you don't. In the long run, tears are a good sign.

You know yourself better than anyone else knows you. If you aren't given to tears in general, you may not cry at a time of loss. If you don't feel like crying in the first few hours or days, don't worry about it! If after some time you feel like crying but can't, seek professional help. A good rule of thumb is, if you haven't "let it all out" after three months, you probably should seek counseling.

Caring for Yourself after the Death of a Loved One

Take special care of yourself in the wake of any major loss. Start with the following seven steps to help you through this difficult time:

1. Assess your state of health before your loss. If you have been under a doctor's care recently, or if you have a history of heart problems, stroke, high blood pressure, or any other serious health problem, get in touch with your doctor now.

2. Be careful about what you eat and drink. Food may not interest you at all. Nevertheless, you need all the energy and emotional strength you can muster. Going long periods of time without eating, then consuming foods with little or

> If you haven't "let it all out" after three months, probably you should seek counseling.

no nutritional value, or drinking large quantities of beverages with caffeine or alcohol is not good. See Appendix A for nutrition guidelines.

3. Talk about the deceased person. Talk with anyone and everyone who will listen to you. Reminisce about past good times and tell stories that are unique to the one who has died. Do not hesitate to talk about the events surrounding the death. You may find yourself telling the story of how the death occurred over and over. That's normal and good.

4. Make time for solitude. Before the funeral at some point, take time to be alone. Dedicate at least an hour to this important task. Say out loud to yourself: "_____ is dead; he (or she) is dead." Don't say *gone* or *passed away* or *passed on*. Use the word *dead*. You need to hear yourself say it. Don't be afraid of your emotions. Not even hysteria will hurt you.

5. Keep your normal routine intact as much as possible. Go to bed as close to your normal bedtime as possible, even if you don't feel like sleeping. Avoid tranquilizing yourself with medication, drugs, or alcohol.

6. Allow your community to help you. This may be your church, synagogue, friends at work, or members of a lodge, a club, or any other group outside of your family. Many people won't know what to say, but that doesn't matter. Their presence is what counts. It's nice to let them know that.

> Don't say "gone" or "passed away" or "passed on." Use the word "dead." You need to hear yourself say it.

You may find that prayer and other religious practices do not come easily. That, too, is normal. In the first hours, you may even forget the name of your rabbi, priest, or minister. Again, don't worry about it. Your faith will catch up with you along the way.

7. Allow yourself to have angry feelings. If you find yourself angry at the world in general and at God in particular, it's okay to feel those emotions. It won't hurt the world, God, or you! Remember: Even if you know the answers, it is always okay to ask "why?"

Organizing the Funeral

The funeral typically takes place three to five days after a death. However, delays may occur because of the cause of death, the distance family members have to travel, weather, and availability of a facility and someone to officiate. That's okay.

Your time for the next few days will be consumed with decision making. If you are responsible for making arrangements, you have to

- Select a mortuary.
- Make decisions about the date and time of the funeral.
- Decide whether the casket will be open or closed.
- Decide whether to have a memorial service without the casket present.
- Make arrangements for the body to be buried in an earthen grave or above-ground crypt.
- Choose embalming or cremation. If cremation is chosen, decide if the cremains are to be buried, placed in a niche, or scattered.
- Select someone to officiate at the funeral. In most cases that will be a priest, rabbi, or minister.
- Make seemingly endless phone calls, each of which is just as hard to make as the one before it.
- Locate insurance papers, birth certificates, and military records, if any.
- In some circumstances, decide if there is to be an autopsy.
- Arrange to obtain copies of the death certificate.

You probably will not want to do any of this, but it must be done. You might find all the activity to be a blessing in disguise. Friends of the deceased or relatives who have no demands made upon them often find it is harder to cope in the first few days than do friends or family who have assumed responsibility for making the arrangements. For many people, making funeral arrangements and doing the other necessary tasks gives structure to an unstructured time and provides some clarity at a time when everything else seems so unreal.

One mother found comfort in dressing the body of her thirteen-year-old son for his funeral. She was at work when he shot himself accidentally with his father's handgun. She had felt helpless from the time the news reached her. Dressing him, she said, provided the first sense of being able to do something for her son. She did not want strangers to perform this intimate task, and it allowed her to touch him and "fix" him as she had done when he was a little boy.

It isn't fair to have to make decisions with long-term consequences (such as the cost of the funeral) when you are in a poor mental state. But making a disposition of the body and doing something about a funeral won't wait until you feel better. At this time, a trusted outsider can be a tremendous help. Don't hesitate to call on a friend to help you with these decisions or to act as a sounding board while you work out for yourself what to do. You could also call on a neighbor, clergy, or counselor. Ask this person to go with you to the mortuary, help select a casket, and assemble clothing for the funeral, if needed. If you must drive a car during the first few days, be very careful. You will be easily distracted and your reaction time may be considerably slower than normal.

> If you must drive a car during the first few days, be very careful.

The funeral director can also help with many details and offer good counsel. I have heard stories about unscrupulous morticians who take advantage of people in crisis, but in more than thirty years of being involved with funerals, I have never encountered such a person. The funeral directors I know are honest businesspeople who have a genuine concern for their customers.

Viewing the Body

You may have to decide whether to view the body of the deceased before or at the funeral, or whether to view the body at all. If you prefer, you can choose a private family viewing before anyone else arrives to allow time to get over the initial shock and be more in control in public.

There is only one hard and fast rule about viewing the body: *Do whatever you feel like doing or not doing.* There is no right or wrong way to do it. Many people find that viewing the body prior to the service helps them comprehend the reality of the death. Seeing the body of your loved one in a casket makes it difficult to run and hide from the loss. It also can bring a sense of comfort if you were not present when your loved one died, or if that person had suffered a lingering, debilitating illness and now appears at peace.

My mother-in-law was a victim of Parkinson's disease for many years. Her mind remained sharp, but the disease ravaged her body. In later years, she struggled with constant pain. When she died, my wife and I both found comfort in how relaxed and at ease she appeared at last.

It isn't wrong to touch the body. When my wife's brother was killed, she was not able to accept the reality of his death and begin mourning until we went to the funeral home and she touched him. If you have never touched a dead body, it helps relieve the initial shock if you know that the body will feel very cold to you and the skin has a somewhat leathery texture.

> It isn't wrong to touch the body. Choosing not to view the body is okay, too.

Choosing not to view the body is okay, too. You may want to remember the person as you last saw him or her. It may be that the circumstances surrounding the death make it impossible or undesirable for you to view the body. If you have heart problems or high blood pressure, it may be preferable for you to deal with the loss more slowly.

Whatever you decide is perfectly okay as long as it is not a way of denying the death. If you can't decide what to do and are in good physical health, I suggest you view the body in private, then decide what you want to do at the funeral.

The Day of the Funeral

The day of the funeral is unlike any other. If you are a family member, you are the center of attention. You may think the whole world is watching you suffer. The only good thing that happens at the time of a loved one's death is that your extended family gathers for a reunion. Telling stories, recalling the past, and giving each other support can provide you with a special measure of strength.

Many religious communities bring food for the family on the day of the funeral. This relieves the pressure on you to take care of feeding people after the funeral. If anybody offers to provide food, accept. I suggest limiting the number of dessert items. Neither you nor your family needs a "sugar fix" during this time of extreme stress. Excessive sugar can give you a boost for an hour or two, but a rapid drop in energy and mood inevitably follows.

> If anybody offers to provide food, accept.

Avoid Drugs and Tranquilizers

Don't take tranquilizers, drugs, or alcohol before the funeral. The service is designed to help you more than it is to do anything for the deceased. To get the most help from the funeral, you need to

- Be as aware as possible of what is happening.
- Be in touch with your feelings.
- Express your grief.

The funeral may be the first time the death becomes real for you. As painful as this moment is, experiencing the reality of your loss at the funeral can be quite important to you a few weeks or months down the road because the only way out of grief is through it (see chapter 7).

Also remember that neither you nor anyone in your family needs to be strong for each other—or for friends and community—at this time. This is not the time to play *Marvelous Christian*, *Noble Jew*, or *Super Trouper*. It is not your job to show how well you can care for everyone else.

First Response to Divorce

The death of a family member is not the only loss that triggers grief and mourning. What do you do when the loss is one of divorce? That announcement is no less shocking than that of a death.

Suppose you have been reasonably happy in your marriage. It has not been all peaches and cream, but then, whose marriage is? One day, out of the blue, your spouse announces that he or she wants a divorce.

Or suppose you have been unhappy in your marriage for several years. Perhaps you have "hung in there" because of the children, or maybe you hoped that one day the relationship would be different. Now it has become intolerable to go on with the charade. You have gathered your courage. Tonight you will tell your spouse that you want a divorce.

Whether you are the one who initiates the divorce or the one who is shocked by your spouse's decision, divorce represents a major loss. Regardless of the side you find yourself on, a number of questions surface when a divorce is imminent. You may wonder

- Can I cope with my feelings of failure?
- Am I doing the right thing?
- How can this be happening to me?
- What will our friends think?
- How can I face my family?
- Can't I just wake up and this will be over?

In a divorce, it is not a person who has died but a relationship and memories from your wedding day. Despite the number of divorces that happen in our society, I have yet to perform a wedding in which the bride and groom expected anything less than a lifetime of marriage.

Acknowledging that your marriage has failed is very much like hearing that your spouse is dead. Some divorced persons have told me they think it is worse!

Sally spoke for many when she said, "If my husband were dead I would at least have a body to bury and something I could do. This way, he is still walking around and I have only my pride to bury. If I were a widow, I would get sympathy from our friends. As a divorcée, I get blamed for it!"

> In a divorce, it is not a person who has died but a relationship and memories from your wedding day.

Caring for Yourself after Divorce

The first seven days after the announcement of a divorce is a time when you would do well to take special care of yourself. I recommend the following:

1. Assess your own state of health prior to your divorce or separation. Yes, this is the same as the first step after a death. If you are under a doctor's care, or have a history of heart problems or high blood pressure, contact your doctor right away.

2. Be careful of what you eat and drink. Yes, this suggestion is the same, too. You may want to respond to your anger and emotional upheaval by going on a food or alcohol binge. The desire is understandable, but the results are not helpful.

3. Find someone with whom you can talk freely. What you need more than anything right now is an understanding ear. Find a person who will listen without making judgments or offering too much advice, someone who genuinely cares about you. It is important to talk about how the decision to divorce happened. Did you make the decision? Or did your spouse drop the bomb on you? What are your feelings? Talking about it is crucial!

4. Don't keep your divorce secret. Let family, friends, clergy, fellow employees, and business associates know your situation as soon as possible. The fear of other people's rejection is almost always worse than reality. The sooner you can be open about what is happening, the better. You have nothing to be ashamed of. If family members, friends, or clergy don't understand, it's their problem!

5. Don't give immediate feelings long-lasting importance. If you are like most divorcing people, your emotions will run the gamut between anger and panic. If you were the one to make the decision to file for divorce, you may go through a period of sheer euphoria. If you had no idea that a breakup was coming, you may feel betrayed and crushed.

Try to remember that you won't always feel as you do now. If you are high, you will probably experience a sudden drop along the way. If you feel torn apart, you will recover.

6. Seek legal advice and emotional or spiritual help. Get both before you make decisions that can't be changed. I can't begin to tell you the amount of unnecessary grief I have seen people bring themselves because they acted on their own volatile emotions instead of seeking legal counsel.

Likewise, everyone I have known who has come out of a divorce truly on top of life has benefited from good psychological and spiritual counseling. When children are involved, this step is an absolute must.

Responding to Other Losses

What do you do when they say the word *fired?* Or the words *cancer, amputation, moving, early retirement, bankruptcy, senility, failure,* or any word that identifies a loss of self-esteem, love, familiar surroundings, or security?

Without doubt, some losses will affect you more than others, but all losses do affect you. Whenever you experience loss of any kind, doing the following will help put you on the right track through your grief.

1. Identify precisely what you have lost. For instance, in a bankruptcy the loss of money or income often is not as traumatic as the loss of self-esteem or self-confidence.

Make a list of the loss or losses. (One major loss may imply a number of associated losses. This is discussed in more detail in chapter 6, starting on page 65.) Identify the feelings you have about each by using the list of feeling words in Appendix B. Which loss calls forth the strongest feelings? That's the one with which to begin your list.

2. Take a personal assessment. What is your physical, emotional, intellectual, and spiritual condition *right now?*

These dimensions of your being are not isolated from each other. Your attitude affects your emotions, your emotions affect you physically, and your physical condition affects both your emotions and attitude. Your spiritual outlook affects everything else.

In which areas do you need help? Identify the best source of help for you in that area. You might need counseling or just a vacation. Follow up on seeking whatever help you need.

3. Talk about your loss and your grief. Tell anyone who will listen to you about your loss. Tell as many people as you can. Don't hesitate to call your reaction by its correct name: grief.

Set a goal to tell at least one or two people about your loss every day for the first week. Keep a journal of whom you talked to about your loss and the date you talked with them.

4. Find a supportive community. You need people who will support you for the duration of your grief, whether that means a few days or several years.

If you belong to a church or synagogue, you have a ready-made source of support. Your religious community either has an existing support group or needs one. You can be sure there are other people waiting for someone like you to call a group together.

If you are not part of a religious community, you can find a church or synagogue that has such a group, or look for people in your neighborhood, service club, or workplace. If you can't locate an existing support group, you may have to create one. It's not as difficult as you may think.

Loss and grief are universal human experiences. Many others around you need the support as much as you do. Reaching out can be difficult when you are struggling with grief. But you will be rewarded with a strong network of support that makes the path through grief easier.

The Deafening Sound of Silence

For some days following the death of a loved one, you will be surrounded by caring family members and friends. But all too soon the day comes when family members must return to their own lives, and friends seem too weary of coping with your grief.

> The initial shock of one woman's loss wore off at about the same time her support system went home.

If you are divorcing, friends and family will rally to your side and be ready to listen to your complaints and comfort your tears—for a few days. Then they will go back to their own lives and expect you to get on with yours.

Two weeks after her husband's death, Marjorie said, "One day you are the center of attention and it seems everybody cares about you and shares your loss. You wake up the next day and everybody is gone. You are more alone than you have ever been in your entire life. It is so quiet that the silence is deafening." The initial shock of Marjorie's loss had worn off at about the same time her support system went home.

Those of us in churches and synagogues have failed people by pouring out compassion and care for about a week when someone dies—and then disappearing like fog before the rising sun. Being with people through the funeral is good. But it is *after* the funeral that the real work of grief recovery begins—and lasts for a long time. Three years or more is not unreasonable or abnormal.

Preparing for the Weeks Ahead

> It is *after* the funeral that the real work of grief recovery begins—and lasts for a long time.

After any major loss, you may have a difficult time reaching out for help. People will tell you to call them whenever you need them. At the moment you need them the most, the thought of calling others may never cross your mind! You will feel lonely and confused. You will wish somebody would come along to do something without your having to ask.

Most of the time, no one will come. It doesn't mean no one cares. It simply reflects the truth that not many people understand loss and grief. It is time for you to begin taking charge.

Write the following information on a notepad and put it next to your telephone. By writing down this information and keeping it by your telephone, you don't have to remember names or telephone numbers in an emergency or when you are distraught. It is also a way of beginning to take charge of your life again.

1. Name and telephone number of your minister, priest, or rabbi. If you haven't had regular contact with a clergyperson, use the one who officiated at the funeral. If that isn't feasible, think of the emotionally strongest and most understanding person you know. Put that person's name on the pad.

In the case of divorce, do the same. Ask yourself who has been divorced and seemed to grow through the experience. Test the reliability of this source of help by calling that person *before* you really need him or her. Ask if you can call during the night in a crisis. Remember, a "no" answer doesn't mean you are rejected. It means that the other person is either overstressed, is not able to cope with grief, or has some other valid reason for being unable to respond to your request.

During the winter months I looked after about four thousand people in my congregation. There was no way I could always be available to everybody. I was fortunate to have three associates and a group of specially trained laypersons to help carry the load. Still, occasionally I had to say "no" when I was asked for my time.

If your first choice can't help you, call the next person on your list. Once you have connected with someone who is available, be sure you

- Never call at an inconvenient hour unless it is a crisis time for you, and
- Never hesitate to call when you do have a need.

2. Name and telephone numbers of your doctor, including the after-hours number and address and telephone number of the nearest hospital.

3. Names and telephone numbers of family members with whom you can talk the most freely. These should be the relatives you would want notified in the case of any emergency.

Back to Work

If you are employed, go back to work as soon as you can. Let the appropriate people know that for the next few weeks or months, you may not function as efficiently as you did before. Assure these people—your supervisor, business associates, or other contacts—that your performance will return to normal, and believe yourself that it will!

At times you may find that a day is going along reasonably smoothly when suddenly something calls you back to the intensity of your loss and grief. At that point you will need to go home or take a break until you can regain your composure.

It is not uncommon to think you see your deceased loved one in a crowd or hear him or her in another room. An ad on radio or television can recall a poignant memory. So can a song or the conversation of fellow employees. Normal events like these can trigger a barrage of tears. Those with whom you work need to know that it doesn't mean you are falling apart. On the contrary, your tears are a sign of your recovery process.

Changes at Home

Going home to an empty house can be terrifying. So can being at home waiting for your loved one to pull into the driveway at the usual time and suddenly remembering that this beloved person isn't coming home now or ever. Parents who have lost young children to death may have an especially hard time at the hour of their child's nap or bath, or when other children are coming home from school.

Many people report that it helps to have the radio or TV playing when they get home. They use these diversions to distract themselves from former routines. "Don't let the house be completely quiet unless you are ready to deal with your feelings" is the frequent advice given in our grief support group by those who have been there.

"Don't let the house be completely quiet unless you are ready to deal with you feelings," say those who have been there.

You may find it difficult to leave the house. Facing the world again as a widowed or divorced person is a strange sensation. One widow had not driven a car for ten years before her husband's death. When he died, she had to learn again. Not only was it frightening to face traffic, but each time she got behind the wheel she was reminded that she was there only because her husband was dead. For several months her grief intensified each time she drove.

Changes with Divorce

The divorcing person has most of the same things to face as the widowed person, plus others. Widowed people get sympathy in the early going at least, but few friends or relatives will seem to care how much your divorce hurts.

The divorced husband typically relocates, usually to an apartment. Housekeeping, meals, and laundry can be real problems. People seem to expect that every male who gets divorced is overjoyed at gaining his "freedom" and can hardly wait to start playing around. Actually, most of the men I talk with are scared of re-entering the dating scene. Their grief at losing their marriage and family is often intense.

> The divorcing person has most of the same things to face as the widowed person, plus others.

Women with young children have the awesome task of becoming single parents and trying to meet the needs of their youngsters without much help. Typically a divorce is costly enough that the family home must be sold, both persons must work, and childcare must be arranged. The standard of living often declines dramatically.

Like everyone else who experiences grief, you will have to face some challenges for which you are not ready. Sometimes you will think you are the only one ever to have felt what you are feeling right now. You may think you are losing your mind. You may wish that you could run away or die. You will feel as lonely as you have felt in your entire life.

Hear this message: You are normal! What is happening is to be expected. It is a necessary step through grief. It must be faced. It will pass. You will conquer this thing.

3

Getting Back on Your Feet

Recovering your balance

Recovering from a major loss is not like getting over the flu. Grief is not an illness. It doesn't help to take two aspirin, go to bed, and wait for the grief to go away. When you experience a major loss, it is as though the rug of life has been jerked out from under you. Someone or something that gave life meaning and joy for you is gone forever. You don't know which way to turn or what to do. Getting back on your feet is a difficult but important first move toward recovery. It can take much longer than you expect to feel "normal" again.

The Urge to Escape

More people than I like to remember have tried to medicate their way through grief. It never works, but I have to admit it's tempting. It isn't difficult to find a doctor who is willing to prescribe tranquilizers for the first few days or weeks. The problem is that being tranquilized can create a fog around your emotions and block the beginning of grief recovery.

Taking medication is sometimes necessary, but it should always be the last resort. If depression persists for weeks or if anxiety attacks are frequent and severe, it is time to seek professional intervention. The issue is one of *intent*. Medications that are taken to keep from facing the reality of the loss do more harm than good. To take control of your grief, you must face your loss directly, with all your senses and your mind working. You can't do that while you are blissfully tranquilized—any more than you can safely drive a car while under the influence of alcohol.

However, it is also true that antidepressants can give you needed strength to make the decisions that will take you to recovery. Hundreds of people with whom I have counseled have used antidepressants in the course of their grief recovery with no apparent negative effects. Getting back on your feet after a major loss is one of the most difficult tasks you will ever face. There is no more shame in using "a crutch" to accomplish this task than using one to recover from a broken leg.

The Challenge of Getting Up Again

After the death of a loved one, the shock of divorce, or the disillusionment of bankruptcy, people often say something like "It knocked me flat." It is not an overstatement but rather an accurate description of experiencing a major loss. You are affected emotionally, physically, and spiritually. You will feel disoriented, uncertain, and weak in the knees. You may feel so tired that even *thinking* requires tremendous effort. Your religious faith may seem as shattered as your life appears to be. Many people have reported how difficult it was to go back to church. Memory losses and forgetfulness are almost universal.

> Medications that are taken to keep from facing the reality of the loss do more harm than good.

Other family relationships are often affected in dramatic ways.

- A divorce can result in confused loyalties among family members.
- The death of a child produces incredible stress between the parents.
- Parents and siblings of a deceased child often struggle with their feelings about each other.
- The death of a spouse can make it seem as if no family member really matters—or cares.

No One Response Fits All People

Janet's husband, Dan, left for work at the same time that he always did. It would have been like any other day if she hadn't received a telephone call an hour later from a sheriff's deputy. Dan was only two miles from home when an eighteen-wheel truck turned in front of him. Dan died instantly.

Janet was filled with disbelief and horror. She was sure it was a mistake and Dan would call to say he was okay. But Dan didn't call. Weeks after the funeral, Janet would find herself going to the door and looking for him. Then the anger set in. She filed a lawsuit against the trucking company. I'm convinced that it was the energy of her anger that sustained her over the next two years. It gave her a reason to get up in the morning and a purpose for living. In time, the lawsuit was settled and her life began to take on some sense of normalcy again.

Mary was driving a group of neighborhood children to the ice-cream store. Somewhere along the way, her own toddler choked to death in the backseat. Mary was unaware of any problem until she arrived at their destination.

On the day of the funeral, the family called me to say Mary was hyperventilating. As soon as she could breathe again, she would begin screaming hysterically until her breath was once more gone. Family members had tried everything to get her calmed down, without success. I went to the house and ordered everyone out of the room, except for Mary.

When we were alone, I told her that I was there to be with her, that I understood the immensity of her loss and her sense of guilt. I said, "Mary, you can respond any way you want to this terrible thing. It's okay with me if you hyperventilate, scream, throw-up, wet your pants—anything that will help you get through the funeral this afternoon. I won't let you be harmed, and there are plenty of people who love you who will clean up any messes."

She looked me squarely in the eyes for a long time—I think to see if I really meant what I said. I did not take my eyes off her and tried not to blink any more than I had to. She threw her arms around my neck, sobbing not in hysteria, but in an anguish that was totally appropriate to the loss of her baby. Later, after the funeral, she could not remember being out of control, only that she felt better after my arrival.

Dan was an engineer who designed computer hardware and programs. His work was brilliant in part because of his skills and in part because he never let his emotions guide his response to any challenge. When his son was murdered, Dan conducted interviews and press conferences without a tear in his eyes. We never sat down in chairs so I could "counsel" with him. We walked, sometimes for miles at a time, while he talked about his son's death—never about his own feelings. His response seemed to break all the rules of good grief recovery process, but it worked for him. This was the way he functioned normally, and he did not vary from it under the stress of grief. He went on to make a full recovery and leads a full life today.

It isn't better to remain calm like Dan, angry like Janet, or hysterical like Mary. There was nothing wrong with the way any of them reacted to their losses. They all responded in ways that helped protect their shattered lives and emotions. Each of them was beginning to recover long before being aware of it.

You will react to a major loss in your life in ways you can't predict ahead of time. It will seem as if the foundations of your very existence have crumbled. Before you can pick up the pieces and get back on your feet, you will need to regain your sense of balance.

It's an enormous task that takes time.

Think back to some loss in your life.

- Remember how your life seemed to crumble.
- Write down some of the feelings you had at that time. See Appendix B for a list of words that describe feelings.
- With whom did you talk about those feelings?

If you are like most of us, you kept most of your thoughts and feelings to yourself.

Trust Yourself

Loss and grief are subjects we should be talking about frequently—before losses occur. The fact is that we have not been talking about these experiences very much, even after the losses. Because of this conspiracy of silence, the task of grief recovery is made more difficult. We think there is something wrong with a perfectly normal reaction, such as intense crying or bitter anger.

The most frequent statement I hear from people in grief support groups is, "You mean other people do that? I thought I was the only one and that I was going crazy!" Actually, a very small percentage of people experience mental illness after a major loss, but almost everyone does "crazy" things. When a loved one has died (even a pet), you may struggle with issues of security, self-esteem, and depression. You will do and think things that seem strange to you and, perhaps, to others. This is one of those times in life when "weird" means normal.

> A very small percentage of people experience mental illness after a major loss, but almost everyone does "crazy" things.

Forgetfulness

You may find that you have forgotten how to do tasks that had been routine. Sue was a secretary who regularly typed eighty words per minute with flawless accuracy. A month after her divorce, she complained she could not type her own name without making a mistake. When my grandmother had to give up living alone and moved in with us, she forgot that our coffeepot was electric and put it on the stove burner. By the time the odor of burning plastic reached us, it was destroyed. I had my own introduction to this phenomenon when we moved to a different state after thirty-three years of being in the same area. In the next six months, I locked my keys in the car four times.

Whenever I meet with a group of bereaved persons, we inevitably spend some time laughing at ourselves for our forgetfulness. What's happening is the emotional equivalent to overloading an electrical circuit. Our minds and emotions can absorb just so much stress and then they "short-out." That isn't a bad thing. I see it as a protective mechanism, an automatic reflex that functions like a fuse or circuit breaker. It's a necessary step for most of us that enables our emotional resources to gain strength for the difficult task of grief recovery.

Keys and Phone Numbers

It is normal to be forgetful in the first several months after a major loss. "Veterans" who have been dealing with grief for a while tell newly bereaved people to guard against locking themselves out of their cars and houses. They suggest keeping an extra set of car keys in a magnetic box placed discreetly out of sight, or better yet, acquiring a remote entry device. It's always a good idea to have a trusted neighbor keep a spare set of house keys.

Another important idea is to write down needed telephone numbers, including the most familiar ones. Place a copy of the list by the telephone and carry another on your person.

This advice applies to any major loss, not just to the death of a loved one. Forgetfulness hits almost everyone regardless of the source of grief.

You will continue to recover your emotional balance as time goes on and you gain more skills in coping with your loss. The more you understand that what is happening to you is normal, the less forgetfulness and other common occurrences will frighten you. Take hope and comfort in knowing others behave in the same ways.

The following exercise has been well tested by thousands of people. It can help you begin to recover your emotional balance and get back on your feet.

Write each of the following statements on a separate piece of paper in your own handwriting. (Don't type them or use a computer.) Make three copies.

- I will not always feel as I do now.
- I am doing okay. Grief will not destroy me.
- I will make it through this experience just as others have before me.

Post one copy of each on the door of your refrigerator. Put another in your bathroom, either on the mirror you use most frequently or on the lid of your toilet. (You will use these household items regularly, regardless of your grief.) Keep the third copy with you.

Every time you see these statements, read them aloud. Keep reading them until you know them by heart and the words come automatically in times of special sadness. Being forgetful is only another aspect of your grief experience, just like sadness, fatigue, and anger. It is a sign of your movement along the pathway to recovery. You aren't falling apart; you are coming together.

> You aren't falling apart; you are coming together.

In spite of your feelings to the contrary, you won't always feel as you do early on in the process. You will recover your balance, get back on your feet, and have a good life.

Tears

On your journey to recovery, you will shed more tears than you thought your body could hold. Four months after her husband's death, one widow said, "Now I understand why they say the human body is mostly water. I've cried enough tears to fill a swimming pool!"

> I am a big believer in tears.

I am a big believer in tears. There is a sign near the door to my office that reads, "People and Tears Are Welcome Here." There is always at least one full box of tissues in plain sight and more nearby. When someone comes to talk about a pending divorce, the death of a loved one, or a child who has run away, I want that person to feel free to cry as much as needed. When our grief support group meets, there are always boxes of tissues around the circle in highly visible locations. The tears of a newcomer or "veteran" are met with a casually passed box of tissues. The clear message is, "Your tears are okay here."

I am among the men who have grown up believing that "big boys don't cry." I don't know who ever taught us that bit of foolishness, but we never should have listened. Women are smarter and healthier, not weaker, because they typically have an easier time crying. The two best things men have going for them these days is (1) being in the delivery room when their children are born; and (2) watching massive football players weep openly when they have lost a game. Being present to the birth process softens them up, and it doesn't take a rocket scientist to conclude that if the *really* big boys can cry, so can I.

Tears can be embarrassing if they flow in public. They most certainly turn your eyes red and make your face look puffy. But those are the only negative aspects of crying. Crying is actually one of the healthiest things anyone can do. Studies have shown that tears of sadness have a different chemical makeup than tears of joy. Tears of sadness release substances that have a calming effect. It is no myth that you will feel better after a good cry. Some studies indicate they are also washing toxins out of the body—which means not crying is holding these poisons inside.

Add this to your list of notes to be posted around the house: *Tears are a sign that you are on the way to recovery.*

Jack came to see me a few months after his wife died of a heart attack while they were on a skiing trip. He had been absent from church since her death. In the past, the two of them rarely missed a Sunday. He told me he had reached the church door several times but just couldn't come in. He would begin to cry uncontrollably as the memories rushed over him of having Helen beside him and listening to her sing the hymns. Each time he tried to come he would get a step or two inside the door, then turn around and go home to cry alone. He didn't want anyone to see him "acting like a sissy."

As we talked, I discovered that he wasn't sleeping well and was eating infrequently. He also reported that he was having occasional chest pains and shortness of breath.

I suggested to Jack that his unwillingness to cry was hurting him and blocking his ability to get back on his feet after Helen's death. It may sound unkind, but I scolded him for his foolish pride that kept him away from church and for his lack of confidence in the rest of us to be able to understand his grief.

I told him our church Cry Room at the back of the sanctuary was not only for parents with babies but also for adults who did not want to cry in public. I urged him to join the grief support group where he could talk and cry with people who would understand perfectly. Jack accepted both suggestions.

He used the Cry Room for a few weeks and then rejoined the rest of the congregation. Without doing anything else, he began to sleep better and eat better. His chest pains disappeared, and in time his physical health was back to normal.

The Pattern of Recovery

Getting back on your feet after a major loss will follow a fairly predictable pattern—which may seem like the pattern of a crazy quilt. You need to know this. It isn't as though you will ride an escalator from the basement of grief to the penthouse of recovery. Neither is it like climbing a set of stairs with a firm tread and a good, solid handrail.

If you are like most of us, you will have times when your recovery seems like a hopeless maze with no way out. Sometimes, moving forward will seem to you like slipping backward. About the time you have some part of your grief figured out, a new challenge is likely to appear.

The best image I can think of to describe the pattern of grief recovery is to picture yourself trying to walk the greased tracks of a roller coaster in the dark . . . in a wind-driven rainstorm . . . with lightening flashing all around. It's frightening. It's almost impossible to figure out which way is up and which is down. You think you will fall at any moment. You take three steps forward and slip back two. It feels terribly "messy" and uncomfortable. But in the end, you make it.

Like Jack, you will be able to cope with your losses and grief better if you have some idea of what to expect of yourself on the journey to recovery. You need to know that

- Forgetfulness is common, and it doesn't last.
- Tears are a sign of healing.
- You are not alone in your feelings.
- Grief takes time—a lot of it.
- You will move through various stages of recovery.
- If you know what to look for, there are visible signs of progress.

Any loss is upsetting. It isn't only death that can knock you off your feet. Divorce, relocation, financial loss, chronic illness, and children leaving home are among many other experiences that can devastate your life.

> Recovery takes time, attention, and hard work.

These kinds of experiences are part of being a human being in a mortal, frail, imperfect world. They happen to everybody. They knock you off balance, leaving you feeling flattened and defeated. You must recover your balance and get back on your feet before life can go on. This is the task of grief recovery.

This recovery takes time, attention, and hard work. If you don't take the time to pay attention to your grief and do the work it calls for, life after a major loss will never again be as full as it could be.

But in the end you will make it. You will stand tall. You will reach your destination. You will know that you have achieved a significant victory. Life will be whole again.

4

Sudden Loss or Prolonged Loss?

Shock or fatigue?

A major loss can happen in one of two ways: suddenly or gradually. In the long run, the grief process is about the same. At the very beginning, however, your reaction to the loss will be different depending on whether the loss happened in the blink of an eye or over time.

Typical sudden losses include the death of a loved one by a heart attack, an accident, or murder. Prolonged losses include the death of a loved one after months or years of struggling with cancer, pulmonary disease, Parkinson's disease, or Alzheimer's. Death by suicide is in a class by itself. It happens suddenly, but threats or attempts to commit suicide may have occurred for quite a while before that.

Sometimes a divorce has been "brewing" for years. When the marriage ends, no one is surprised. Other times, one partner's announcement that the marriage is over catches everyone off-guard. It is not unusual for one person to contemplate a divorce for years while the other person in the marriage is blissfully unaware of the impending crisis.

There is no easy way to lose someone dear to you or something meaningful to you.

Just about any other major loss experience you can think of—job loss, relocation, loss of good health—may happen suddenly or slowly.

All major losses are painful beyond words and require an adjustment period. The appropriate response in every case is grief. There is no easy way to lose someone dear to you or something meaningful to you. However, it may appear as though *any* other way would be less painful than the way you have experienced your loss. If the death was sudden, you wish there had been time to get used to the idea. If the loss was prolonged, you are sure a quick death would have been less painful for all concerned.

The first time I met Ted and Laurie was to plan a funeral for their twenty-seven-year-old son. He had been living at home with his parents while he paid off some debts that were overwhelming him. The end of the task was in sight as he and his girlfriend made plans for their future—and bought a little dog. He worked at his parents' restaurant where he enjoyed the work and the people all enjoyed him.

Ted was at work, leaving Laurie and their son at home alone, when the young man locked the door to his room, placed towels on his bed—and shot himself. There was no warning, no indication of added stress or depression, and no explanation.

Ted and Laurie joined our grief support group as they struggled to make sense of a seemingly senseless tragedy. They looked for some sign they might have missed or something they could have done to prevent his death.

It took months for them to work through the shock and understand there was no sign and there was nothing anyone could have done to keep their son alive. His suicide was a decision that he made for reasons that will never be known.

They continue to make their way through their grief in a healthy and appropriate way. The recovery of Ted and Laurie seems certain, though life will never be quite the same for them.

Diane had to cope with a different challenge. Her husband, Allen, had his first heart attack in 1977. For the next twenty-one years, his recurrent health problems dominated their lives. He had other heart attacks, bypass surgery, angioplasty, stents installed, and he required numerous medications. In 1997, Allen was diagnosed with cancer.

I lost count of the number of emergency trips I made to hospitals, each time thinking this was probably when Allen would die. But he always came back, not merely to survive, but to live a life of reasonably good quality. Diane's early response to his death was, "I hardly know what to do with my time, now that he's gone. His health needs have dictated what I do every day for twenty-one years."

Like many survivors who have cared for a chronically ill person for a long time, Diane experiences a certain sense of guilt for the freedom she feels. She is no longer under constant pressure to be aware of Allen's condition, even at night. She can go where she wants, when she wants. Yet it's hard for Diane to enjoy her freedom because there is only one reason she isn't under the same old pressure: Allen is dead.

Both Ted and Laurie and Diane have to establish new lives now. Each had a different initial response to their loss. But after the first few months, their experiences will even out, and they will probably follow a similar pattern of mourning and recovering from their grief.

The Special Dynamics of Sudden Loss

A sudden loss is a momentary incident that changes your life forever.

Don and Sally were delighted that their only son was going from Arizona to Michigan to play with a concert orchestra. Their excitement turned to shock when the commercial jet on which he was flying crashed in a snowstorm, killing everyone on board. Their grief is still evident several years later.

The special dynamics with which Don and Sally have had to cope are typical of sudden losses.

1. Lack of preparation. There was no chance to say "good-bye," "I'm sorry," or "I love you." These parents had no forewarning of what would happen and were not prepared for it. Their son was healthy, talented, and successful. At eighteen, he had a bright future. Don and Sally's hopes and dreams for their son did not include the possibility of an untimely death.

When losses happen suddenly, we have a horrible sense that "I need time to be ready for this and I'm not going to get it." Complicating the emotional aspects may be practical ones. For example, perhaps one person in a family has always handled the finances, and he or she dies suddenly. The survivor has to cope with the new challenge of taking care of the pocketbook at a time when he or she is least able to do so.

Common wisdom says we can never adequately prepare for any major loss. That's true under any circumstance, but the reality is all the sharper when the loss occurs suddenly.

If you experienced a sudden and catastrophic loss, you may believe that if only you had had the chance to prepare for it, your loss would be easier to face. No one would argue with you . . . except the person whose loss occurred over months or years.

2. Difficulty accepting reality. The unreal nature of a death, divorce, or job loss is magnified if that loss happens suddenly. Questions are urgent and intense and usually begin with "why." Don and Sally have not been able to resolve the "why" of their son's death, although several years have passed. Like most survivors of sudden loss, they found themselves expecting their son to return at any moment.

You may wake up in the morning, hoping to find you have been dreaming, only to realize yet again that what happened is no dream. Your loss is real, and it is permanent.

3. Anger. Virtually every bereaved person is angry. The difference for survivors of sudden loss is that they are more aware of their anger, and it is often more intense than it is for those whose losses are prolonged. If responsibility for the loss can be identified, the anger will also be more focused. Don and Sally are angry with the airline company for flying in bad weather. They would be angry with the pilot, but he also died in the crash.

Frequently I hear people express anger at doctors and other medical people for not saving their loved ones. The tacit assumption is that if the medical professionals had done their jobs, the person would not have died. When sudden losses occur, it's as if we revert to that point in childhood where *somebody* must be to blame

Virtually every bereaved person is angry.

for any unfortunate incident. By contrast, those who cope with a prolonged loss have time to work through the blaming phase. They come to understand that people die, even with the very best and most talented medical help.

If yours was a sudden loss, it's important for you to know that the anger you feel is normal. It's also important that you find a creative way to release your anger by granting forgiveness or by making peace with the flawed and frail nature of this mortal life. A trusted friend, your minister or rabbi, or a counselor may be able to help you get to that point.

4. Guilt. The two most frequently used words by those who experience a sudden loss are *if only*. "*If only* I had done something different." "*If only* I had been more aware of his symptoms." "*If only* I had called 911 sooner." "*If only* we had talked more, this divorce would not be happening."

Jean was driving the family car when she and her husband were involved in an accident. The accident killed her husband instantly. Jean's list of "if only's" is almost endless.

The issue is *guilt*. Guilt is the flip side of blaming someone else for the loss. With guilt, we blame ourselves. When it appears, guilt is typically more intense for survivors if their loved one's death was sudden than if the death was expected.

5. Secondary anxieties. If a death happens suddenly, survivors are left to wonder, "Did my loved one suffer?" "Was he or she frightened?" Often I hear people in grief support groups agonize over what might have been going through their loved one's mind just before the incident that caused the death. Secondary anxieties can be pervasive and long-lasting.

My parents died six months apart. Each of them was alone at the time of death. That was forty-one years ago. At times I still wonder what they were thinking and feeling.

I have been present when dozens of persons stopped breathing and died. I have seen their family members remain free of the kind of anxiety that is felt when no one is present and the person dies alone.

My granddaughter, Carrie, was driving on a freeway late at night when she spotted an object in the lane ahead. As she swerved to avoid it, she was shocked to see it was a person, down on the freeway. She stopped and ran back to find a badly injured young woman. Others stopped and began to wave off oncoming cars as Carrie knelt beside the victim and comforted her. The young woman tried to speak but could only mumble incoherently. Seeing fright in the woman's eyes, Carrie wrapped her arms around her and held her. The young woman died in Carrie's arms. In the months that followed, the parents of the young woman called Carrie frequently to ask about their daughter. Had she been in pain? Did she seem frightened? They invited Carrie to their home for dinner and expressed a deep gratitude to her. The fact that their daughter had not died alone on the street was a great comfort to both of them.

Other questions survivors ask frequently are, "Can we view the body?" "Are there photographs?" and "Did the deceased person say anything to anyone before death?" These and questions like them are ways survivors use to understand what happened and to make contact with the event retroactively.

If your loss happened suddenly, be assured that your reactions, however bizarre they may seem to you, are probably no more extreme than those of anyone else who has had a similar experience. Sudden loss has its own special dynamics, and none of us has been trained in how to cope with the experience.

You will be okay! Over the long road of grief recovery, your experience is neither easier nor more difficult than if your loss had been prolonged. You will find much in common with others who have had similar losses. You *can* recover your balance and move on with your life.

When Loss Is Prolonged

Not all losses happen abruptly. In fact, most losses happen in a period of months to years.

The word that seems to describe this experience best is *fatigue*. While you may feel deep shock when the illness or situation is first disclosed, that feeling is eventually buried under the incredible burden of coping with prolonged loss. Emotions soar and fall with every hopeful or discouraging development. When all is said and done, prolonged loss involves just as much grieving and feelings of emptiness as sudden loss. There is the same terrible finality to contend with. But some aspects of the adjustment are different in the first months.

> Prolonged loss involves just as much grieving and feelings of emptiness as sudden loss.

Guilt and Prolonged Loss

People who care for a dying person for a prolonged period sometimes struggle with guilt. Typically their guilt is not nearly as intense as it is when the death happened suddenly. The most common expression of guilt I hear after a prolonged illness has to do with the survivor not being present when death finally comes.

Irene cared for her husband for more than fifty years of marriage. He had a stroke and was in a coma in the hospital for more than two weeks. She was there all day, every day. She had gone home for much needed sleep on the night he died. Irene has struggled with guilt for not being there when the moment of death came.

I was called to a hospital to visit a woman who was gravely ill. Arliss had struggled with pulmonary disease for several years. She was now at a place where it seemed as if any quality of life was impossible. Her survival was in jeopardy. Her lungs continued to fail for reasons that weren't showing up on tests.

Her husband, Marty, sat by her side, holding her hand, stroking her hair, and offering words of love and encouragement. He appeared as calm as he did strong—until you looked into his eyes. When Arliss was sleeping under the effects of medication, I said, "Marty, you look tired." He responded, "I've never been more mentally, emotionally, and physically exhausted in my life."

By day's end, he heard the awful truth: Arliss was dying. She went home a day or two later and went under the care of hospice.

Marty's experience with a prolonged loss is different yet bears some similarity to Don and Sally's experience with a sudden loss. Don and Sally had to deal with shock. Marty had to deal with fatigue. Both situations are extremely difficult. The level of grief Marty will face when Arliss dies will be every bit as deep as that of Don and Sally. It will take a long time for all of them to recover.

The Role of Hospice

In recent years the emergence of hospice has been a wonderful development for the physical comfort and emotional care of those who are dying and of their loved ones. Hospice is a medically directed, team-managed service program that focuses care on the patient and family. Professional and volunteer hospice workers provide not only good medical and social services, but they also bring the added benefits of dignity for the one who is dying and compassion for his or her family.

Hospice care is palliative rather than curative, with an emphasis on pain and symptom control, so that a person may live the last days of life fully, with dignity and comfort. Palliative care frees the patient, the family, and medical personnel to talk openly about the end of life. Many times, dying people are able to help survivors make decisions. Funeral arrangements can be made, plans for a surviving spouse's support can be put in place, and family and friends can visit. Perhaps the most significant part is that all of this can be done with the person living at home or in a home-like setting at a hospice facility.

In most cases, hospice workers are prepared to stay involved with the family for as long as a year.

When death occurs, the hospice workers are either present or arrive within minutes. They take over contacting the funeral home and arranging for transportation of the body.

In most cases, hospice workers are prepared to stay involved with the family for as long as a year. Their comfort level with the subject of death and grief provides strength and stability for the survivors, especially when other family members and friends begin to depart. They can greatly soften the "thud" that comes with being alone with grief for the first time.

Chances are there is a hospice group near you. Check your telephone book, call your hospital, or ask a librarian at your local library for reference help. Hospice organizations have my highest endorsement (and admiration).

Prolonged Loss in Divorce

I don't know of any hospice-type group for dying marriages, but we could use one. It isn't easy to find a pastor or other counselor who is willing to counsel for divorce. The focus always seems to be on doing something to save the marriage, not on finding ways to allow it to die peacefully.

Jean and Joe were married for seventeen years. They had three children. Throughout most of those years, one or the other, or both, were unhappy. They didn't fight. They weren't mean to each other. There were few harsh words. They just didn't fit well together in terms of what it took for each to feel fulfilled. For the last seven years of their marriage, Jean grew increasingly despondent. She tried to stay in it for the children, their parents, and as some kind of act of contrition. It didn't work. Finally, she told Joe she was leaving and filed for a divorce.

Fortunately, Jean and Joe were counseled by a sensitive professional who understood that the dynamics between them were incompatible. Families who supported each of them without blaming anyone helped both Jean and Joe through the process.

Jean and Joe held hands as they filed their divorcing papers. They went through the process without lawyers or court appearances. They agreed on joint custody of the children and an equitable sharing of assets and liabilities.

> Families who supported each of them without blaming anyone helped both Jean and Joe through the process.

They both continued to attend school and church functions that involved the children. Birthdays and holidays were celebrated with both parents present.

In time, first Jean and then Joe remarried. The two couples meet regularly and have become good friends. In fact, Jean's second husband was a groomsman at Joe's second marriage. The lack of stress and the sense of security in the children is readily visible.

Jean and Joe have demonstrated that it is possible to go through the dissolution of a marriage, with emotional pain as severe as any death, and still maintain dignity and respect for each other. Another divorced woman commented to Jean that her relationship with Joe was "weird." Jean's reply was, "No, what we have is normal. It's the other way that is weird." Joe and Jean have fully recovered from their loss and have moved on to very happy lives.

Common Factors of Sudden and Prolonged Loss

Once initial adjustments are made, the grief process takes the same path, whether a loss was sudden or prolonged. Grief is finally grief, whatever its cause. The length of time required, the work to be done, the "mileposts" that mark your progress and what it takes to have life be full again are the same.

> Grief is finally grief, whatever its cause.

The shock of sudden loss wears off with time and effective grief work. The fatigue of prolonged loss typically doesn't last long. Loneliness is every survivor's long-term adversary.

No matter how difficult circumstances may seem to you right now, believe this: There is no "easier" way your loss could have happened. However your loss occurred, acknowledge it as "the way it is" and take charge of your grief. Keep going. Talk to people.

5

Steps to Recovery

Walking the path to wholeness

Recovering from a major loss is like being forced through a twisting maze that presents you with one dead-end after another. To complete the journey successfully requires perseverance more than anything else. Put another way, life seems shattered in a million pieces, and your challenge is to make it whole again.

How any of us experiences grief varies as widely as our personalities and life histories. Picture yourself as one of twenty people in a group dealing with grief. Each person is asked to ink his or her thumb on an ink pad and then make a thumb print on a piece of white newsprint fastened to the wall. When everyone has completed the task, all would agree that you were looking at a lot of thumb prints. Nevertheless, no two of them would be exactly the same. The same is true for grief: No two people experience it exactly the same way.

However, you can expect to take certain steps along the path to recovered wholeness that are similar for everyone who is recovering from a loss. Some of these steps will seem automatic—out of your control. Others will require enormous willpower to finish. Some steps may take a few weeks to accomplish; others could take three years or more.

Understanding these steps will help you deal more effectively with grief. You will know you are making progress, even when it feels as if you are slipping backward. You will not have the added burden of thinking something is wrong with you when actually you are reacting in a normal way. You will be able to describe your experiences to family and friends and tell them how they can support you most helpfully.

The steps are:

- Shock and numbness
- Denial and withdrawal
- Acknowledgment and pain
- Adaptation and renewal

1. *Shock and Numbness*

In the first seven to ten days after a major loss you will probably feel stunned, shocked, and overwhelmed. You may feel "frozen"—or hysterical. Either way, you will have a difficult time later remembering much of what took place.

Whatever your initial outward reaction, you will have a certain numbness inside. Your emotional system has shut down for the time being. I like to think of it as God or nature supplying us with temporary protection against the full impact of our losses. The experience of shock provides us with a brief, sheltered rest before we begin the long journey through the agony of grief toward a renewed sense of joy.

> This is a poor time to make decisions that will have a lasting impact on your life.

A few days after the death of a loved one, when the funeral is over and relatives have gone home, the shock begins to wear off. This is a good time to have someone with you. It is a poor time to make decisions that will have a lasting impact on your life. People who give away clothing and possessions, decide to move from their homes, or quit jobs within a few weeks of a loved one's death often regret those decisions.

In the case of divorce, the shock comes either with the announcement by one spouse to the other of the desire for a divorce, or the actual filing.

I answered the phone one day to hear the familiar voice of my dear friend Jim. He was calling from another state. His voice was hushed as he said, "Bob, Marge wants a divorce. She doesn't want to be married to me anymore. I keep saying this can't be happening to us, that I'll wake up any minute—I can't believe it!"

Now it was my turn to be shocked. June and I had known Jim and Marge for more than twelve years. We had shared many family experiences together. I thought I knew them as well as anyone in my own family. They were the last couple I would have expected to divorce.

I mumbled something to Jim about telling me what happened, but I don't remember what he said after that. My mind was racing back over the long hours June and I had spent with Jim and Marge over the years, talking about future plans—the mythical restaurant we had planned in the greatest detail, the trips we would take, sharing our children's weddings. None of this would happen now. For June and me, the shock of losing our friends as a married couple was magnified by the loss of the dream we had for the future. I found I could not approach this divorce with any sense of professional detachment.

For Jim and Marge, the shock came in facing the reality of their lost dreams. Children loved by both had to live in separate homes. There was property to divide. Friends and family had to be told. It wasn't the way they had planned their lives.

Jim and Marge taught me that the shock and grief that comes with divorce is not less than that which comes with death. It takes the same week or so for the shock to wear off. And it takes much longer than that to complete the recovery.

> The shock attached to relocating comes when we first confront the strangeness of our new environment.

The shock attached to relocating comes when we first confront the strangeness of our new environment. A young couple came to my office one day in tears. With their baby, they had arrived in town a few days earlier. Everything had seemed okay. They had a place to live. Their belongings had arrived undamaged. His new job would start on Monday.

But on that particular morning the baby awakened with a fever. All of a sudden the shock hit: They didn't know where to begin looking for a doctor in this large city. They had come from a town with one percent of our population. Back home they knew the doctor, the druggist, and even the mayor on a first-name basis. This wasn't home, and they felt lost.

Other loss experiences have a similar effect. You may have been cool and collected as you prepared for surgery and then found yourself "coming unglued" as you were being prepared for the operating room. The realization that "it" is really going to happen can stun the strongest among us.

Shock follows every loss experience to some degree. The important things for you to know about shock are:

- It is a necessary first step to recovery.
- It doesn't last long.
- It is not a time for long-term decision making.
- It is good to have a trusted friend with you.
- When shock goes away, pain arrives.

2. *Denial and Withdrawal*

When the shock of your loss wears off, you will want to deny what has happened with all your strength.

No one can begin to describe the incredible depth of pain we feel when a loved one dies. If you have already had that experience, you understand. If you haven't lost someone to death, think about another very painful personal loss you have had. A pet's death can be very painful. People grieve over lost friendships, mourn the move from familiar places, and agonize over bitter disappointments in their lives.

As unavoidable and natural as loss is, we are seldom ready to admit that loss is a normal part of our own life. No one plans on a divorce at the time of marriage. When we think about relocating, we are usually more aware of new places to be seen than old ones to be lost. We seldom stop to think that *our* parents, spouses, or children are going to die someday—and that the loss of these important people can be within our own lifetime.

It's natural to deny a loss when to acknowledge it leads to so much pain. After an initial reaction of "Oh, no!" what is most significant about this step may be what is happening *without our being aware of it*. Behavior and attitudes may change for a while. Health may suffer, too.

Physical and emotional effects you may experience after the initial shock of the loss wears off include:

- Feeling weak and drained of energy
- Inability to perform routine tasks
- Lack of appetite
- Lack of sleep or oversleeping
- A persistent dry mouth
- Physical aches and pains
- Lack of concern with personal hygiene or grooming
- Fantasies of the deceased or divorced person
- Expecting a dead or divorced person to come back
- Disillusionment with your new city or home
- Anger

These are all normal reactions to loss. You may experience one or several at a time. It's possible you will think you are done with one reaction and weeks or even months later it will return.

> Repeat these words: "I will not always feel like this."

If you know to expect these signs of denial and withdrawal after a loss, you can comfort yourself by saying, "This reaction is normal. This is another step on the way through grief. I will not always feel like this." I have seen many people recover energy for the task of grieving simply from repeating words like these to themselves.

In this phase, disappointment with family and friends may surface. Your closest friends and members of your immediate family may not respond to your grief in ways that are helpful. Even those who know you best will not understand your grief any better than you do. Well-meaning people who really care about you will want you to "be okay" much more quickly than you can be. Most won't know what to say. Some people will avoid you. Reactions like these aren't unusual, and you aren't alone if you experience any of them from friends or family members.

At the same time, you may be too fatigued to ask for help. Even making a telephone call can seem like an insurmountable task. You will want others to reach out to you, but you will not be able to tell them what to do or say to help.

You will want to tell the story of your loss again and again. You may find that the world around you will be through listening long before you are through with the need to talk. Some will "reward" you with kind words and more frequent visits if you pretend to be on top of things. It won't seem to matter to them that you really feel as though you are dying inside.

> You will want to tell the story of your loss again and again.

If you understand that conflicts such as these are normal, you can be more patient with others—and with yourself. This is especially helpful when anger surges within you during this phase, either because of such conflicts with others or because you want to blame *someone* for your loss.

Linda came into our grief support group two months after her husband's death. She was filled with anger, blaming everyone for his death, including herself. She wrote a letter to herself as an exercise that appears on the opposite page.

The anger and blame in Linda's letter may be unreasonable, but little is reasonable about grief at this point in the recovery journey. Read the letter again and picture some hurtful loss of your own as you do. Change the names and circumstances to fit your experience. See if Linda didn't express feelings and anguish that you have also felt. These kinds of angry reactions are signs of your denial of the loss. They are a symbol of your mind's effort to withdraw from the pain. It isn't wrong to have these reactions. It may even be necessary for your survival in the early months after a major loss.

Dear Linda,

Did you do all you possibly could to help Earl? Do you believe everything a doctor says? Don't you know that most doctors are in it for the money and not to help people? They took the easy way out with Earl. All they wanted was their thirty pieces of silver!

Linda, don't you think you should have noticed Earl's health more? Instead of going for a walk with him, you could have taken him to a heart specialist. You say you didn't know anything was wrong. Why not? If you had been a little more observant, my partner Death and I would not have paid you a visit.

Sincerely,
Grief

Denial and withdrawal is a difficult phase of recovery because you are least able to reach out when you most need to do so. Others are also least able to help at the time you most need it. The more you know about the step of denial and withdrawal, the less isolated and helpless you will feel. Be assured this phase will pass.

3. Acknowledgment and Pain

The classic term psychologists use for this stage is acceptance and pain. I do not refer to this step as acceptance because of Ann. She joined our grief support group after her husband choked to death in his sleep. I was talking about accepting our losses one day when Ann broke in to say, "Bob, the word acceptance carries with it some sense of approval and there is no way I will ever approve of my husband's death. I'm ready to acknowledge that he is dead and he isn't coming back, but I refuse to accept or approve it!" Every person in every group I have talked with since agrees with Ann.

> Acknowledging a loss is the most important step of your recovery.

Acknowledging a loss is the most important step of your recovery. It is at this point that you will again take full charge of your life and full responsibility for your feelings. A noticeable sense of balance is coming back into your life when you can acknowledge that your loss is real—and permanent. It represents a giant step toward full recovery.

If you have had a loss through death or divorce, you will probably be ready to acknowledge your loss fully in about three to six months. However, if it takes you a year or more to get to this point, you won't be the first. Nor will it mean you aren't doing as well as someone else. Everyone reaches this stage of grief at his or her own pace.

When Rae joined our grief support group, it had been eighteen months since her husband's death. When asked why she had decided to join at this particular time, she replied, "I thought I was doing fine. I handled the funeral okay and went to work shortly afterward. I was lonely at times, especially in the evenings. But all in all I thought I was doing pretty well. In the last month, it's as if I'm right back at the beginning. I didn't cry the first time around, but now I cry all the time."

Rae had not been ready to acknowledge her husband's death "the first time around." Now she was. It was important for Rae to see she was not going backward, but forward, because she was crying now. She wasn't "worse" than she had been for eighteen months, she was *better*. She was ready to move on. In the months that followed, she did just that.

If you have never endured a major loss in your life, you may not be able to understand the depth of pain that acknowledging such a loss can bring. My wife June has had two major surgeries, both of which were in response to life-threatening illnesses. Both surgical procedures made lifetime changes in her physical body. I have had back surgery once. There was no threat to my life. In fact, the quality of my life was improved by the procedure. I can remain naïve about facing the possibility of my death. June cannot. Her feelings of complete vulnerability going into surgery are different than my experience.

Grief is like that. It takes you into new territory. When I first started meeting with a group of widows, I had to say to them, "You are the experts here. I am an amateur. My parents have died, my brother-in-law died at age six, I have moved to a strange city, and all my children have left home. These losses I can understand. But I don't know what it feels like to have my spouse die, and furthermore, I don't want to know! You will have to tell me about that experience, and I will try to understand." Twenty-five years and countless grief-support-group meetings later, I am still listening and trying to understand. When my wife was diagnosed with breast cancer and we waited to see if it had spread, it was as if the door to the experience of losing her was opened just a crack. For a few days I could see just a tiny bit of what it would feel like if she died. I probably learned more in those few days than in all the years of careful listening to those who fully experienced that nightmare.

There is nothing easy about saying "I am divorced" or "My child is dead" or "This part of my life is over." It hurts!

This is an up-and-down phase.

But it won't hurt forever. Emotional pain is another sign of your progress toward a full life. It is important at this point of your recovery to remind yourself—often—that you will not always feel as you do at this moment.

You will be tempted to slip back into denial of what has happened. You can do that periodically and you will feel better—for a little while. But the only pathway to balance and wholeness lies through the pain of the acknowledgment of your loss.

A support group or professional counseling can help a lot in this phase of your recovery. People around you will ask, "How are you?" They expect to hear that you are "fine," regardless of how you actually feel. If you *aren't* fine and you tell the truth, many people will ignore your words and behave as though you hadn't said a thing. Then you may feel worse than you did before.

A counselor or a support group can give you the opportunity to talk freely and get your feelings off your chest. You can be sure that your counselor or others in the support group will hear you and understand you. You need little else right now as much as that un-derstanding! The acknowledgment phase is a long one, and for that

Those who have been there assure the rest of us that slowly but surely, the good days begin to out-number the bad ones.

reason it is extremely important that you have a strong support system in place as you find your way through it.

This is an up-and-down phase. You will not stay immersed in agony for a year and then suddenly wake up one morning to find yourself finished with it. You will make progress one day and encounter difficulties the next, but overall you will be heading in the right direction. Those who have been there assure the rest of us that slowly but surely, the good days begin to outnumber the bad ones.

4. Adaptation and Renewal

The first sign that the roughest part of your grief is over will be when you notice a change in the questions you ask yourself. From the time of your loss, the most haunting and persistent question is, "Why did this happen to me?" The day will come, often a year or more after the loss, when a new question will emerge. That question is, "How can I grow through this tragic event to become a better person?"

When you stop asking "why?" and begin asking "how?" you are beginning to adapt to your new life without the person, place, or condition that has been lost.

Elizabeth came to our grief support group at the urging of a friend. She was as angry about her husband's death as anyone I have ever met. For several months, she had nothing positive to say. She was angry at the doctors, the insurance company, family, and anybody else she could think of, including God. I'm sure it seemed to Elizabeth as if no one had ever grieved as deeply as she.

Slowly, however, she changed and her outlook became more positive. She became the source for some of the best laughter experienced in the group. She brought in clippings and quotes that were meaningful to everyone. On some occasions, she filled in as group leader in my absence. She is now the person newcomers in the group turn to most often.

Today Elizabeth works at ways to make her life as enjoyable as possible. She is adapting to her loss and emerging as a new person in her own right. I think she even likes her "new" self better than the former one!

"Why?" Questions

The worst thing about "why?" questions is that they have no satisfactory answers. Questions that begin with "why" reflect a desperate yearning for meaning and purpose in your loss. It seems so unfair. You are sure there is some reason for what happened. You think you might feel better and hurt less if only you could discover that reason.

Lois's son was playing golf when he was struck by lightning and killed instantly. Four young men were standing together when the fatal bolt struck. Her son just happened to be the tallest of the group. For months the one question that dominated Lois's mind was, "Why Derek? He was happily married, had a great job with a great future. Why him?"

- Why did I get this cancer?
- Why did my husband die when he was such a good man and others who don't care about their families live?
- Why did my wife want someone else when I've provided so well for her?
- Why did we have to move to this godforsaken place?

"How?" Questions

Questions that begin with "how" indicate you are ready to face the reality of your loss. They also express your search for ways to put together a life after the loss.

Pauline's mother died in May. A year later her son died in the same month. Two years later her husband also died in May. When she came to the grief support group more than a year after his death, she said, "I had to wait until I was finished asking 'why?' before I could come. I reached a point where I had to move on with my life or die. I have come here to find out how I can keep going."

These questions touch on issues such as

- How can I fill the void in my life that my wife's death has left?
- How can I learn to compensate for the hand I injured in the accident?
- How do I learn from my divorce so I won't make the same mistakes again?
- How can we make friends in our new city so we will feel more at home?

It is certainly difficult for us to accept that some things, even deaths, happen for no purpose. It's easy to forget the word "accident" means just that—something that happens because this is not a perfect world with a perfect script written for life.

When your questions begin to change from "why?" to "how?" you are beginning to accept that accidents include your own tragic loss.

I want you to be able to say this with confidence:

The loss I experienced is a major event in my life. Perhaps it is the worst thing that will ever happen to me. But it is not the end of my life. I can still have a full and rewarding life. Grief has taught me much, and I will use it to be a better person than I was before my loss.

These words are not easy to say. It isn't easy to think these thoughts after a major loss. It is even more difficult to say the words aloud. You can't rush them. But working toward saying them with conviction is a reasonable goal.

When you can acknowledge these truths about your loss, you will find a renewed energy and enthusiasm for life. You will begin to adapt to a new life that does not revolve around your loss experience and grief. You will have a new sense of self-worth. If you are like most people, you will find a new calmness within yourself. Little things won't irritate you as much. You will take yourself less seriously, and you will laugh more.

This is a good time to obey an urge to try a new hairstyle or wardrobe—or both! It may be a good time to redecorate a room or take a trip. It's time to establish new goals for yourself over the next two to five years.

As time goes on you will realize that recovery is a lifelong process of adapting to all kinds of changes and losses. As with any ability, you will get better at this as you continue to use the skills you have learned from this loss. You won't forget your loss. It will always be a part of your life history. But in time you will be able to think about the person, the place, or the condition that was lost to you without pain.

The day will come when you will know deep inside that you have recovered your balance, completed your journey through grief, and are ready to get on with a good and full life. On that day, you will be a stronger person than you have ever been before.

Healthy versus Distorted Grief

Grief is the nuclear energy of our emotions. Understood, respected, harnessed, and directed, it can be a creative force. However, when grief is out of control, distorted, and misunderstood, it can become a destructive force.

It is important, therefore, to recognize when your grief is healthy and when it is distorted. If you have a common cold, you know how to care for it. You don't need a doctor or a hospital. But if your cold becomes pneumonia, it would be foolish not to seek professional help. So it is with grief.

As you have read through the steps to recovery that I have described in this chapter, I hope you found your fears diminishing. I hope you learned more about what to expect from yourself as you experience healthy grief. Reactions and feelings that may have frightened you are in most cases normal under these extreme circumstances, and they will pass. However, I also want you to know some signs of distorted grief.

Five Symptoms of Stress Overload

Here is a list of five symptoms that indicate you have had all the stress you can handle alone. The presence of any of these symptoms says it is time to call in professional help. Remember: There is no shame in seeking help. The only shame would be to need help and not get it.

1. Persistent thoughts of self-destruction. The key word is *persistent*. It is not unusual to have suicidal thoughts while experiencing grief, but they should pass quickly. If you begin thinking of a specific method and occasion for taking your life, seek help. The key decision for healthy grief is, "I will live."

2. Failure to provide for basic needs. If you find yourself changing your patterns of activity and avoiding friends and family, it is time to seek help. Interaction with other people is essential to healthy grief.

Equally important is paying attention to your physical needs, including nutrition, fluids, exercise, and rest. If you are failing to take care of these fundamental needs, it is time to seek help.

3. Persistence of one particular reaction to grief. Depression that immobilizes you for weeks is a sign professional help is needed; so is continued denial of the reality of your loss, or finding yourself still without feelings months later. Help is needed when any normal grief reactions persist too long.

4. Substance abuse. This means everything from using tranquilizers or sleeping pills for too long, to engaging in alcohol or drug abuse. It also includes eating too much, too little, or surviving on junk food.

5. Mental illness. Persistent feelings of anxiety, hallucinations, or a collapse of body functions indicates emotional breakdown. A good rule of thumb: Any time you are unable to function normally, seek professional help.

> There is no shame in seeking help. The only shame would be to need help and not get it.

If you are "on the fence" about seeking psychological help—get it! Your minister, priest, or rabbi can refer you to someone who specializes in grief counseling. When you first contact a counselor, don't hesitate to ask if he or she has experience working with grief. You will know within one or two sessions whether the person will be helpful. If you sense that person does not have a good understanding of your grief process, try another counselor.

6

The Inward Search

Grief is a personal experience

Any major loss is first and foremost a personal experience. Your loss is yours, regardless of how many other people are affected by it. Because of this, it will be difficult (it may seem impossible) to share your feelings with others. It will be equally difficult for anyone else to understand what's going on inside of you.

To recover your balance and to get back on your feet will require you to search within yourself for strength and hope. No one else will be able to give you satisfactory answers to the questions that dominate your thoughts.

Your journey through grief will have many aspects in common with others who have also had terrible losses. But you will not respond exactly like any other person. You are a unique person, and your grieving will reflect your uniqueness.

A perfectly normal reaction to a major loss is the conviction that "no one else has ever felt as I do." There is a sense in which that is true. Bereaved people tell me that having another person say, " I know how you feel," is much worse than the sound of fingernails across a chalkboard—especially if that person has not had a similar loss. Nobody knows exactly how you are feeling, including your family and closest friends.

If your spouse has died, you are concerned about other family members. If you have divorced, you may worry about the welfare of your children. After a business failure, you may care about other investors or employees. But your first concern—what will dominate your feelings—is the sense of *personal loss*.

You will not ask, "Why has this happened to us?" You will ask, "Why has this happened to *me?*" Others can offer help and encouragement, but only you can take charge of your grief and your recovery. Only you can decide if your loss will be an occasion for growth in addition to being a time of grief.

Think of a loss you experienced in the past. If that loss was severe enough, it became the center of your life experience. As far as you were concerned, it didn't matter if the sun was shining brightly. To you the days were dark and gloomy. It did no good for some well-meaning person to try to cheer you up with reminders of all the reasons you had to be thankful. Your loved one was gone, that place called *home* was far away, or your dream was shattered. You were in no mood for platitudes.

In your heart it was pouring rain—and the sadness was about to leak out of your eyes. The orders you gave yourself to calm down didn't work. You had lost something or someone very important to you. That loss hurt beyond words.

The thing you wanted more than anything else was a glimmer of hope. You wanted to know if there was a light at the end of the misery tunnel. If there was such a light, you wanted to know it was not an oncoming freight train loaded with more sorrow.

You did not look around you for answers because you were sure nobody else understood exactly what you were feeling. No one else could take away your pain. As much as you wanted someone else to come to your rescue, you knew that finally you had to work it out for yourself.

If you have experienced the things I've just described, you understand the true meaning of *personal grief*.

The Importance of Perception

Understanding the personal nature of grief is important. The perceptions you have about your loss and your grief are more important. The role of perception is the number-one factor in successful grief recovery.

Perception means what you "see" from inside your own head. It's the old question of how full or empty the glass is. Picture your life as a glass of water. It used to be full to the brim. Now, some of the water has been spilled and lost. Regardless of how severe your loss or losses, the glass is not empty. The all-important question is: What do you see? Is your life now one-half full or one-half empty? Is it one-quarter full and three-quarters empty? In terms of your future

> The role of perception is the number-one factor in successful grief recovery.

expectations for a good life, how much hope for fullness do you have?

Two women, both named Betty, lost their husbands several years ago. Both men died of cancer after a lengthy struggle. Both widows were left financially secure. Both have families who were supportive. Both were active in their churches and had a wide circle of friends. There, the similarities end.

One of them actively denied the reality of her husband's death. She refused to join a grief support group or to talk about her sorrow with anyone. She became more reclusive as time went on—and more bitter. She kept her husband's military uniform hanging in the closet—as though he were away at sea and would be home any day. Every month, the uniform was sent to the cleaners. She shined his shoes, keeping them neatly arranged under the hanging uniform. This routine of denial was still going on nine years after his death. Betty's own health began to fail as she withdrew ever deeper within herself. The last I knew, she was confined to a nursing home, crippled by arthritis and dementia.

The "other Betty" perceived her loss differently. She joined a grief support group where she talked openly about the anguish of watching her husband die slowly and how empty she felt with him gone. Her tears flowed freely at times, but there was always a glint in her eyes that said, "I am going to overcome this." She divided time between our community in Arizona and the city where she and her husband had lived for several years. My wife and I visited her in that place about two years later. She was active in her church and community. She had again become "life-oriented." During another winter in Arizona, Betty met a

man who had lost his wife at about the same time she had lost her husband. Eventually, I had the privilege of officiating at their wedding.

The major difference in the two Bettys was their perceptions of their
losses.

One became a *victim*, the other a *survivor*.

Victims are passive, feel helpless, and let circumstances dictate their
feelings. Survivors are assertive, take charge, and understand that
whereas they may not be able to control their circumstances, they can
always control their attitudes toward those circumstances.

To successfully cope with your personal grief, you must perceive that

- You will live.
- It's okay for you to have a life after your loss.
- You can take charge of your own grief.
- Although you can learn from the experience of others, strength
  and hope will come from within.
- You can reach the place where there are less tears and more
  laughter.

To "see" these things in the midst of grieving is a real challenge. But
it is possible. Let that perception help you get back on top of life again!

Reflecting on Personal Losses

Put the following questions on separate pieces of paper. Write your answers to them using as many pages as necessary to fully express your
feelings.

- Will I survive the losses I have experienced?
- Is it okay to go on with my life without whomever or whatever
  has been lost to me?
- Can I be happy again knowing that my life will be different because of my losses?

Read your responses aloud to yourself. See what they say about your inner thoughts and feelings.

The more resources you have, including religious beliefs, family traditions, and supportive groups, the more fruitful your inward searching will be. The more you understand what to expect of yourself, the better you will be able to recognize the signs of grief recovery and growth.

On another piece of paper, write the name of your most recent loss—a person's name or "my marriage," "my home," or whatever best describes the loss. Under the heading of your major loss, list the additional things you've lost as a result of it. For instance, if your spouse died, your list might look like this:

> Major loss: *My husband, Joe, died.*
> Resulting losses: *financial security; companionship; may lose home; retirement dreams; close ties with Joe's family; independence; sense of personal value*

The same kinds of things are often lost if you are dealing with divorce instead of death.

Make your list as complete as possible. Take a look at your resulting losses. Do any of them suggest even *more* disappointments? If so, add these to your list.

Notice that whatever loss you experienced caused you to have a *series* of losses. *Each one hurts.* Each one hits at the core of how you measure your happiness and the value of your life.

Bill was thirty-two when his wife committed suicide. He said to me, "I didn't just lose a wife. My sense of self-worth and all my plans for the future went into the ground with her! What do I do now?"

Nancy, whose husband divorced her after twenty-eight years of marriage, said, "When he walked out the door, my security went with him. I've got to find some way to earn a living."

Jack lost everything in a business venture. He said, "I had to learn to see my personal

> Notice that whatever loss you experienced caused you to have a *series* of losses.

value as separate from my dreams of success before I could give up the idea of killing myself."

Minor Losses

Not all of your losses will be as serious as the death of a loved one, a divorce, or a major move. Nevertheless, even so-called "minor" losses can have a far-reaching impact on your life.

After driving safely for thousands of miles, my wife, June, and I had two automobile accidents in less than forty-eight hours. There was no way to avoid either of them. The second was a head-on collision with a truck that crossed the center of the road on a blind curve. June's head hit the windshield. After the impact, I looked at her and saw blood from her face coloring her white pants a bright red.

Within minutes, people who were total strangers had put her in their car to travel to the nearest hospital several miles away. I remained with our car, waiting for the sheriff to arrive. I had no idea how seriously June was injured or how long it would be before we were together again. By the time I realized I didn't even know the names of the men who had taken her away, June was gone from the scene of the accident.

Over the course of our married life, one of June's pet sayings to me has been, "You take good care of me." I have always enjoyed that vote of confidence. As I stood by our wrecked car and sobbed tears of shock and remorse, I kept muttering, "I didn't take care of her. I didn't take care of her. I lied."

I questioned my decision to stop at a market shortly before the accident. I wondered if I could have driven the car differently to avoid the collision. What if June was badly hurt? What would I do if she died?

As I think back to that experience, I can identify several losses:

- My identity as June's protector
- My pride as a skilled driver
- My sense of security
- My belief that tragedy happens only to other people
- My feelings of being in control of life

I felt intense grief simply at having to admit our life circumstances were not always in my control.

Fortunately, June was not seriously injured. Expert surgery left only the faintest mark on her freckled nose. However, even though we were very lucky, it took a year before we recovered from the effects of that single event in our lives.

That loss experience was not a major one. No one died or was permanently injured. The other drivers' insurance paid for car repairs and medical expenses in both instances. We continue to travel by car as much as ever, even though we were victims of another careless driver eight years later, this time leaving both of us with lasting damage. However, that experience too was not a major loss compared to the terrible things that happen to others. Nevertheless, it was important for us to pay attention to the effect these experiences had on our lives.

The failure to recognize the impact of minor losses is one reason people are often so poorly prepared when a major loss occurs. Reflecting on the way that smaller losses affect our life can help us prepare for the inevitable major losses that everyone experiences.

If nothing else, paying attention to smaller losses helps us understand loss is a part of being alive. Look within yourself to reflect on your response to a smaller loss, and you will discover resources that will serve you well in times of major loss. Chapter 20 discusses more about preparing for loss.

7

Four Key Facts about Grief

Building a foundation for recovery

Learning four key facts about grief will help you take control of it. Accepting these facts will help you develop the stamina and patience you need to endure the burden, stress, and duration of your grief. These are the four key facts about grief:

1. The way out of grief is through it.
2. The very worst kind of grief is yours.
3. Grief is hard work.
4. Effective grief work is not done alone.

Learning to work with grief in these ways may feel strange and uncomfortable. These ideas may represent a whole new way for you to think about grief. But in time and with practice, you will find these concepts to be invaluable tools to recovering from your loss and moving on in your life.

1. The Way Out of Grief Is through It

This is the single most important fact for you to learn about grief. If you want to recover from your grief and grow through your loss, you must learn that there are no shortcuts to a good and full life after a major loss. You have to live through grief to resolve it.

Because grief work is so demanding, it's common to look for *any* way to get out of going through it. No one wants to face grief. No one wants to feel the loneliness and heartache it brings. The common tendencies we all have when we experience grief are to

> There are no shortcuts to a good and full life after a major loss.

- Try to avoid it
- Try to get over it quickly

And, when neither of these work . . .

- Try to wait it out

How often have you heard it said, "Time heals"? But it's not the truth! To say time *by itself* heals is like saying "practice makes perfect." Practice does *not* make perfect. It is quite possible to practice a perfect mistake. Only perfect practice makes perfect. The truth is, only effectively working *through* grief, not simply waiting for it to go away, heals the deep wounds and enables you to recover your balance in life.

Maggie said to me about two years after the death of her husband, "I'll never get over it." We were in a grief-support-group meeting. As I turned to her, I heard myself saying, "Maggie, you're absolutely right. You could work for the next fifty years and you won't get over Roy's death. Neither can you get under it or around it. But Maggie, you can always get *through* it!"

If you are tempted to say with Maggie, "I'll never get over it," good for you. You have learned an important truth about grief recovery. To say you have gotten "over" a major loss implies some degree of amnesia. The only way to forget the pain of a loved one's loss is to forget the loved one. I have never yet met the bereaved person who was willing to give up the memories of a loved one in order to avoid the pain of that person's death.

When you lose a loved one, go through the pain of a divorce, or experience some other dramatic change in your life, you do not "get over" it. That person, place, or time of your life will always be a part of you and your personal history.

An old spiritual, although not written about grief specifically, certainly reflects this important truth. It says:

It's so high you can't get over it,
So low you can't get under it,
So wide you can't get around it,
You must go in through the door.

The more significant your loss is, the greater your sense of grief. You will not get over that loss, or under it—nor is there any way around it. You cannot wait it out. You have to go squarely through the middle of it—and the good news is, you *will* come out on the other side. Learning this truth is one key to your grief recovery.

Irma, whose husband died ten years ago, stopped working at her grief about six months after his death. She tried to avoid the sadness by not talking about it. To this day, Irma has never faced her anger at him for dying. As a result, she has suffered physically and mentally. Poor health and numerous phobias plague her. It appears now that Irma will not have any lasting sense of joy for the rest of her life.

If you have been through divorce, you know one of its great illusions is that divorce puts an end to problems between spouses. The fact is, all that usually changes is you no longer live in the same house.

If you and your ex-spouse fought and argued during your marriage, you are likely to fight and argue after your divorce. If you have children together, you will continue relating to each other for the rest of your lives. When your children are grown, there are their weddings to witness, grandchildren to love, and all the big events in their lives that they want both of you to attend.

Life is too short to spend those years continuing the battles that ended your marriage. The way to achieve peace is to go squarely into the grief that follows the end of a marriage. You can only do that by facing feelings that are the most difficult. It has always seemed to me the first casualty in any divorce is the self-esteem of both spouses. This loss alone can knock you flat on your back emotionally. It isn't unusual to need a year or more to *begin* recovering a healthy self-image.

When one couple divorced after sixteen years, the husband was willing to go to a counselor. He worked his way through some very painful discoveries about himself. He learned that he had related to his wife and family in ways that contributed to the breakup of their marriage. He came out of the experience changed for the better. He is more patient and understanding. He does not take himself so seriously. He walks through life with a lighter step than before. He is married again and very happy. For all the sadness it caused at the time, he is able to look back and say that working through his divorce was a good thing. He is grateful it motivated him to grow and change.

His wife, who initiated the divorce, never seemed to face her feelings. She appears to be trying to wait out her sadness. It isn't working. For three years after their divorce she continued to call on her ex-husband for money, household repairs, and emotional support. After he remarried, she moved back into the house they had shared for several years. She seems to be hanging on to symbols of a relationship that is over. She has tried to avoid grieving its loss. In the meantime, the need to grieve just waits—and grows!

To "go through" grief requires stamina and incredible reserves of patience. At some point along the way, you will feel terribly sad, lonely, lost, angry—or all of these. To get in touch with such unpleasant feelings, you have to be convinced there is absolutely no other way out of your grief than straight through the middle of it. You must have a strong sense of purpose and direction.

> To "go through" grief also is to "grow through" grief.

It isn't unusual or abnormal to feel more uncomfortable after confronting your grief. It should be expected. To "go through" grief also is to "grow through" grief. And that is a positive experience.

Many times after one of our grief-support-group meetings one of the participants will call me to say, "I felt worse when I left than when I came in." The caller is often shocked when I respond, "Good for you! It means you're growing."

Feeling better comes a day, a week, or a few months later. If you are working through a major loss and feel comfortable, it's a danger signal. It's time to check to see if you are trying to skirt the flank, dig under, or get over your grief. It's a fact: You can't!

One more time: Going *through* the experience is the only lasting and healthy way *out* of grief.

Throughout this book you will find exercises that provide effective ways to handle the feelings that emerge as you move through your grief and establish a new life after your loss.

2. The Very Worst Kind of Grief Is Yours

Which grief experience is the worst? Is it more difficult for the widow if her husband suddenly and unexpectedly drops dead of a heart attack? Or is it worse if he dies a day at a time from cancer? Is it worse to lose a spouse to death or a marriage through divorce? Is the death of a child the worst of all losses? All of these are irrelevant questions. There is only one very worst kind of grief—and that is yours.

In one winter two disastrous events happened at the same time, each of which affected my life. First, a number of men were killed in a mining accident. My sister called because she knew some of the families. That tragedy made headline news everywhere. The other tragic event was having our fifteen-year-old cat put to sleep.

Can you guess which of those events caused me to cry my eyes out? You guessed it—the cat!

There is scarcely any comparison to be made between the loss of human life and the end of a semi-crippled old cat. But Samantha was my cat. I loved her. She was a permanent part of our history. Her loss was not an academic thing. I didn't look at television or newspaper accounts of her death and say, "That's too bad!" and go on to the sports page. She was mine. Her loss plunged me into grief.

I stood in the front room of our home as my wife drove off with the cat to the veterinarian's office. I couldn't walk into that office and fall apart in tears. Everyone knows big boys, especially professional clergymen, don't do that sort of thing. So . . . I let my wife do it! I held

Samantha briefly, tickling her under the chin in the way she liked so much, then carried her out to the car where June was waiting. As she drove off, I screamed and sobbed, crying out over and over, "I want my kitty. I don't want her to die!"

This was my loss and at that moment, as far as I was concerned, it was the worst thing to happen in the whole world. I didn't want anyone to tell me how great it was that she didn't suffer, or how far beyond a normal life expectancy she had lived.

I have known deeper times of grief—much deeper. A neighbor girl, who grew up spending as much time in our home as her own, committed suicide at nineteen. My mother and father are both dead. I have held the hands of friends as they died, baptized stillborn infants, helped families decide when to disconnect life-support systems, and worked with parents whose children were murdered.

Each of those experiences was painful. Nevertheless, at the moment my cat died, her loss was the very worst kind of grief for me in the whole world.

Think about your own experience. Perhaps you sold one home and bought a new one. You were excited as moving day approached, only to find yourself standing in the empty old house after the last box was gone, overwhelmed with a deep sense of loss and sadness. As one man said, "It is as if you have divorced your house."

That feeling of sadness is grief. And at that moment, for you, it was the very worst kind of grief simply because it was *yours*.

> Never apologize for grieving. Remind yourself as often as needed that the very worst kind of loss is always yours.

The death of even the most aged family member hurts because the loss is yours. Rabbi Earl Grollman's father was past ninety. His health had been poor for years. He was an invalid confined to a rest home. When he died, a well-meaning friend said to Earl, "He had a long and good life. Aren't you glad his suffering is over now?" Earl says he replied in a voice that did not mask his anger, "You don't understand. My *daddy just died!*"

Learn to acknowledge that your loss is worthy of grief. Whatever your experience is, you must endure your very real feelings of sadness and anger on the way to recovering a full life once more. If you are going to come out of grief a better person, you cannot be concerned about how you "ought to" feel on the way through it.

When Phyliss came to our grief support group, she had lost her daughter, son-in-law, and three grandchildren in a bizarre mass murder. Two years later, her husband died of cancer. By contrast, Susan came only because her widower father needed her to bring him. A year later, he died. Susan continued to come alone after the funeral. One day she said, "I feel guilty for feeling so sad. My loss seems so insignificant compared to Phyliss's loss."

That attitude could have been a stumbling block to Susan's grief recovery. It was important for her to know that her grief was just as real as that of Phyliss.

It hurts to lose important persons, places, and things from your life experience. The correct and appropriate response is grief. If you don't acknowledge your loss and begin to work your way through it, even small grief experiences begin to stack up. They become like bills waiting to be paid—and piling up interest.

As long as you tell yourself you shouldn't feel as you do, or pretend you don't hurt, the loss stays with you. Recovery begins when you admit that no matter what other tragedies exist in the world, at this very moment, the very worst kind of grief is yours.

> As long as you tell yourself you shouldn't feel as you do, or pretend you don't hurt, the loss stays with you.

You do not owe an apology to friends, family, or God for grieving the loss of anything or anybody. If others understand, that's nice. If they don't, that's too bad.

The way out of grief is through it. And, the way through it begins by acknowledging that your loss is worthy of grief, even if it's for an old cat.

3. *Grief Is Hard Work*

Making your way through grief is called *doing grief work*. I never fully appreciated what that means until I immersed myself in other people's grief experiences. There is no better way to describe the things you will endure than the word *work*. Grieving is work. It is the most difficult work any of us will ever do.

Viewing grief as work will help you take an active approach to your grief. It will help you avoid trying to wait it out. It will help you refrain from looking to others to be responsible for making you feel whole again.

> Viewing grief as work will help you take an active approach to your grief.

Some tasks you just can't assign to someone else. Nobody can do the work of acknowledging the death of your loved one for you. No one else can take over the very difficult task of saying good-bye and releasing that person, that relationship, that part of your body, or whatever it is you have lost. You must do that for yourself.

The following image helps me understand the work dimension of grief.

Suppose you have had a group of friends over for a spaghetti dinner. It's been a delightful evening, but now your guests have gone home. You walk into your kitchen, and there sit the dishes. Those tomato-sauce-turned-to-glue-covered dishes are one of the truly ugly sights in the world!

You're tired and in the mood for anything but washing dishes. You have two choices: You can leave the mess until morning. Or you can wash the dishes now, regardless of how you feel. If you leave them, the present moment is certainly more pleasant. In fact, the balance of the evening can be delightful, and your night's rest refreshing. But come daylight, *there they are*, uglier than ever!

Now the task is even more difficult. The pleasantness of the dinner party is forgotten as you face the same decision: Wash them now or put off the gruesome task for another time.

If you choose to wash the dishes immediately after dinner, your guests might help you, if you're lucky. At worst, you face a tough evening of cleanup and go to bed exhausted. But come morning, the task is finished. You can go on to the new day basking in the memory of a good evening and the knowledge that your kitchen once again looks sparkling.

Grief work is much like that image. You have work to do at a time when you feel like doing nothing at all. Like those dishes, grief work can be put off. You can feel better for a while by avoiding some feelings and not talking about some things. But the day will come when you awaken to see that your feelings are still there, and things still need to be talked about with someone who understands and cares.

> About 25 percent of those who mourn experience a dramatic decrease in their bodies' immune system six to nine months after their loss.

The longer you wait to attack those feelings, the more difficult and unpleasant grief work becomes. Grief is not an illness. But if you try to avoid grief work, you may well become sick.

Dr. Glen Davidson's research showed that about 25 percent of those who mourn experience a dramatic decrease in their bodies' immune system six to nine months after their loss.[1] That lack of immunity accounts in part for the higher rate of illness when we are grieving. The research also demonstrated that this immune system deficiency could be avoided. If you do the work of grieving, including taking care of your physical and emotional needs, you will be okay.

The first thing you need is a support group with whom you can talk freely. See chapter 18 for more about that. Then you must pay attention to the foods you eat, the amount and kinds of fluids you drink, and getting adequate exercise and sufficient rest.

It's hard work. There is much to do and only you can do much of it. But in other ways you need to share the burden of grieving with others who can help you, as you will see next.

4. *Effective Grief Work Is Not Done Alone*

One of the most hurtful myths you will hear about grief goes like this:

- Grief is such a personal experience that it should be kept to yourself.

Another is:

- Nobody else can help. You have to handle your own grief.

Nothing is further from the truth!

It is another fact of life and loss that effective grief work is not done alone. Your grief should *never* be a private affair. You need other people as much as you need air to breathe. You need to talk about your experiences and your feelings. You need to listen to others share about what's happening to them. There is more than comfort in such sharing. There is the strength you need to endure the length and burden of your grief.

> You need to talk about your experiences and your feelings.

If you keep your grief to yourself, you run an unnecessary risk of it becoming distorted. Mike dropped out of our grief support group after coming twice. He said he wasn't willing to come week after week and cry in front of a bunch of women. The last I knew he was still struggling with blackouts and ulcers. He married again less than a year after his wife's death. His new wife has been to see me several times to talk about his moodiness. Mike refuses to come with her.

Jane could never tell the group that her marriage had not been the idyllic romance she had wanted it to be. Neighbors and friends knew about the loud arguments and alcohol problems. But after her husband's death she talked about their relationship as if it had been made in heaven. After a few months, she became increasingly hostile and unwilling to share her feelings. Her participation in the group was limited to giving advice to others. In time, she dropped out altogether. For a while, she attended other grief groups in the city, none of which satisfied her. Four years after her husband's death, Jane was still a bitter, unhappy person.

The saddest fact about Mike and Jane is their problems could have been avoided. You can move through your grief experience and come out a healthy person. To do that, however, other people must be involved in your life and your grief.

The Power of Shared Experiences

Of all the groups in our church, my favorite is the grief support group. I can't imagine a more sensitive and caring group of people anywhere. Nowhere else have I seen the age barrier disappear more quickly. There is

> The more you talk about your grief work publicly, write about it in letters, and share in the grief of others, the more effectively you will adapt to your own loss.

something very special about seeing a young mother whose baby was stillborn and an eighty-year-old widow taking care of each other.

Those who share such deep places together become a real help to others. They seem to know instinctively the right words to say to a newly bereaved person. They know the time to speak and the time when words are neither adequate nor necessary.

The more social your grief work is, the better you will do with it. The more you talk about your grief work publicly, write about it in letters, and share in the grief of others, the more effectively you will adapt to your own loss. I don't mean to imply it's easy. It is only *necessary*.

Men and Grief

Men seem to have more difficulty sharing grief experiences than women do. Some of this reluctance probably has to do with the masculine dread of emotionalism. Many of us have grown up with the silly notion that tears are a sign of weakness and lack of character. The price for such foolishness has proven to be very high.

A man I know has been on the brink of bankruptcy for several years. In the past he was a successful businessman. He and his family lived in a fine home. His attempt to expand into a new venture led to the loss of their business and their home. They are faced with starting all over again.

Outwardly he seems to be holding up very well. But he doesn't want to talk about his feelings with anyone. He could be growing through his loss. He could be having the strong support of people who would understand his feelings. He could be on his way to recovery. He isn't. In addition, by keeping it all to himself, his risk of serious illness is many times higher than normal.

Men have the same basic needs for healthy grief recovery as women do. This includes the need to be with others who have had similar losses and the need to talk openly about what is happening inside as the result of the loss.

If you are male and have suffered a major loss in your life, don't try to handle it alone. If you are too uncomfortable meeting with a group of women, a little investigation will uncover other men who share your feelings. Get together for breakfast or lunch on a weekly basis. Use this book as a guide for your discussions.

> Like most grieving persons, you will probably come to hate the questions, "How are you?" You will discover very quickly that the only acceptable answer is "fine," regardless of how miserable you are feeling at the moment.

Careless Things People Say

Almost every divorced person and every widow or widower I know has had someone say something that can only be called cruel. Bereaved persons are often rejected for crying and rewarded for keeping a bright smile, even when it is killing them to act happy. Divorced men and women find friends taking sides and making judgments at a time when what they need most is a friendly ear.

Numerous widows have shared experiences with me of being forgotten by social or church groups after the death of their spouses. After her husband's death, Maggie gathered up the courage to go back to a bridge club they had belonged to for several years. It was a difficult step. The bridge club was an activity she and Roy had always shared. When Maggie arrived, she was greeted at the door by a long-time friend who said, "My dear, don't you know this is for couples?"

It doesn't take more than one experience like that to convince you to keep grief to yourself!

You will find people, including some doctors and clergy, who are too uncomfortable with grief to reach out to you. Friends may avoid you because they don't know what to say. Co-workers may be afraid they will say something that upsets you, so they say nothing at all. It often seems that a conspiracy of silence develops whenever you are present.

Nevertheless, it is a fact that effective grief work is not done alone. It is vitally important for you to find a counselor or a support group who will listen, if friends and family aren't up to that task. Almost every community offers such resources simply because loss is a universal human experience. In Appendix C you will find guidelines for forming a grief support group yourself if one is not available.

8

Start Now!

No one else can do it for you

I keep a quotation by an unknown writer pinned to a bulletin board over my desk:

> *There will never be another now—*
> *I'll make the most of today.*
> *There will never be another me—*
> *I'll make the most of myself.*

It's a good motto for doing effective grief work. The only time you have to start working through your losses is *today*. Tomorrow will not be a better day to face the task. The only one who can make the journey through your grief is *you*. But you will discover you are equal to the challenge.

Doing grief work, in one sense, is a little bit like making love—talking about it takes you only so far. And no one else can do it for you.

Admittedly, there is nothing pleasurable about grief. But if you learn the skills of effective grief work, you can emerge from your losses with a renewed sense of confidence.

> Tomorrow won't be a better day to face the task.

There is no better time to start working on grief than right now. If you have experienced a major loss, it won't help to wait for some other day when you feel better to start working on it. The potential risks to

83

your health and the absence of joy from your life are prices too high to pay for postponing the task.

Helpful Exercises

This book contains exercises that can help you handle any loss in your life. Each exercise presents a task that focuses on a specific step to grief recovery. Not all of the exercises will apply to you at this moment. However, all of them are worth your attention.

For instance, exercises on handling grief after divorce also apply to other losses. With minor adjustments, those that focus on death also apply to divorce or relocation. If the particular loss addressed doesn't fit your experience, it may apply to someone you know who needs your understanding and help.

> Doing the exercises will help you continue to move through your grief.

Remember that you will not move through grief in an orderly, well-defined manner. A task that seems completed three months after loss may have to be done again many times. If this is your experience, it is not a setback—it is a perfectly normal way for grief to progress. Doing the exercises will help you continue to move through your grief, toward recovery.

Applying the Four Key Facts to Your Grief

As a warm-up to doing other exercises, copy each of the Four Key Facts about Grief onto separate pieces of paper (see page 85). List one key fact at the top of a sheet, and then list the ways it applies to your grief experience. For instance, write at the top of one sheet, *The way out of grief is through it*. Under this heading, list what you can do to go through your experience and what behaviors to avoid that represent an effort to sidestep your grief. For example, you could remind yourself to talk to someone about your loss every day. You could write a description of the way you feel right now.

Work with the four key facts until you are clear about the way each of them applies to your loss and grief. As you become more comfortable with them, you will be able to see more potential for a full and rewarding life after your loss.

Understanding and accepting these key facts about grief recovery is crucial to building a rewarding life after a major loss.

The Four Key Facts about Grief

For a full discussion of the Four Key Facts about Grief, see pages 69–81.

1. The way out of grief is through it.
2. The very worst kind of grief is yours.
3. Grief is hard work.
4. Effective grief work is not done alone.

A Recent Life History Survey

This exercise is for everybody. It will help you identify loss experiences that may have seemed insignificant at the time they happened, but which could be continuing to affect your happiness today.

Take a survey. Get out a piece of blank paper and a pencil. Answer the survey questions in the sequence in which they are presented. Answer every question before going on to the instructions that follow the survey.

1. List the most significant changes in your life during the past two years. Include positive experiences, such as a job promotion, new home, getting married (or having children married), retirement, or graduating from college. Negative experiences will include a death in the family, divorce, loss of job, surgery, serious illness, moving from familiar surroundings, or business failure.

2. Diagram your moods over the past year: happy (contented); okay (some ups and downs); or sad (depressed, discontented).

	Jan	Feb	Mar	Apr	May	Jun	Jul	Aug	Sep	Oct	Nov	Dec
Happy												
Okay												
Sad												

3. List any physical problems you have had in the last eighteen months.
4. Describe your outlook on life right now in terms of
   • A color
   • A taste
   • A smell
   • Touch
   • A sound

   You might describe life as a dismal gray color, like a foggy, overcast morning. Or perhaps it is a good day, and life is the color of a rainbow. Life could taste bitter or rancid—or as sweet as a ripe strawberry. Life may have the odor of rotting meat, burn your lungs like acrid smoke—or smell like the freshness after a sudden rain. It may have the feel of gritty sandpaper or the softness of a baby's skin. Perhaps your life right now is as noisy as a Los Angeles intersection during rush hour, or maybe it sounds more like a clear stream bubbling over rocks.

   Finding such ways to describe how life looks to you at a given moment is helpful in tracking your progress through grief recovery.
5. Write down the one thing in your life you would change at this moment if you could. (Describe the way you think it is and the way you would like it to be.)

Examine your responses. After you have completed the survey, read over your answers. Examine your responses by doing the following:

1. Ask yourself, "What losses did I experience in each of the major changes I listed?"
2. Ask yourself, "Which of these losses continues to make the greatest impact on my life?" As you think about this loss, what feelings do you have? Refer to the list of feeling words in Appendix B for help in naming your feelings.
3. Check the diagram of your moods over the last year. Is there a correlation between your moods at various times and the loss you have identified? Focus on the saddest of your moods and try to remember what was happening at each of those times. Identify your losses in each of those experiences and name your feelings about them.
4. What was happening during your happiest moods? What feelings can you name about those experiences? In what way were you in control of your own destiny at those times?
5. Look at your list of physical problems. Is there a correlation between these problems and the loss experiences you have named? List the approximate time your physical symptoms were noticed. Measure back six months, nine months, one year, and eighteen months from this time. Note the events in your life around each of these times. Was a loss involved? If so, what was it? Is that loss still affecting your life today?
6. Do your physical problems keep you from doing anything you would do if you didn't have a limitation? If so, describe what you would do if you could. What words describe your sense of loss because you cannot do that particular thing?

   Look at the words you used to describe your present outlook on life. Do you like these images?
   - Is the color your favorite?
   - Is the taste something you like?
   - Is the smell pleasant?
   - Is the touch pleasurable?
   - Is the sound one you would like to hear again?
7. How do you feel about your answers in each category? Do they indicate a positive or negative outlook on life? If your outlook is

more negative than positive, ask yourself, "What have I lost recently that, if it were given back to me, would make my outlook on life more positive?"

8. Think about the thing that you would most like to change in your life. Is it possible to realize that change?

    You can't get back a loved one who has died, a divorced spouse who has remarried, a limb or organ lost to surgery, or a special time in your life. Recovering just about every other loss is possible, regardless of how improbable that recovery might be.

9. If the one change you would make is not possible, you have grief work to do. Identify the focus of your grief. Don't try to fool yourself or name a loss that feels respectable to you. For instance, if you are divorcing and it is not the loss of your spouse that hurts, but the loss of your children or self-esteem, say so. Focus your grief on that loss.

10. If the change you would make is possible, ask yourself, "Why haven't I already made that change? What is holding me back?" Does the change require the participation of someone else? Who? Have you talked with that person about it?

    Knowing that for every change, there is a price to be paid, what is the price for the change you would like to make? Are you willing to pay that price?

Talking It Over

To get the most benefit from the survey, first go through it carefully by yourself and then share your findings with a trusted friend, family member, counselor, or clergy. The simple act of talking about your loss and feelings is an important step to recovery.

Your loss may seem so small that you are embarrassed to make an issue of it. If so, remember the second key fact about grief recovery: The very worst kind of loss is yours.

Pay particular attention to any correlation between your physical problems and a

> The simple act of talking about your loss and feelings is an important step to recovery.

time of loss. You can spend a great deal of time and money treating physical symptoms and never get to its root cause if loss and grief are unacknowledged factors of your illness. If you suspect a connection, you need to see a counselor or clergyperson and a doctor who understand the relationship of grief and illness.

Guidelines for Doing Grief Work

Once you have identified your losses, the next step is to begin the work of recovering your balance. The following guidelines will help get you started and keep you going when you grow weary of the task.

Trust that you will make it through your grief. It is a fact that experiencing grief means you have work to do. It is also a fact that this work has an end point. In the early going I can only ask you to take my word for it. You probably think your sadness will last forever. It won't. That will become evident to you later as you do the exercises I suggest.

> Believe that your grief has a purpose and an end.

Earlier I compared grief work to washing dishes. Once you have washed the dishes, that work is finished until you use the dishes again. Grief work is like that. Once you have done the work required for you to regain your balance, it is finished until you experience another loss. The more you learn about grief, the better you can handle it.

Nobody wants to be good at grieving—we are half-afraid that having such a skill would only attract more grief. We would much prefer to do without the grief experience entirely. But life doesn't work that way. Because you will not be spared from times of loss, it is important to believe that your grief has a purpose.

If your outlook on life is upbeat and healthy, you trust that basically life is good. When you experience a major loss, that basic sense of trust is shaken. You will question whether life is not actually chaotic and unfair. In truth, sometimes it is!

Shortly after our marriage, my wife and I were awakened in the middle of the night in our third-floor apartment by a strong earthquake.

We awoke feeling disoriented and scared to death. The room was swaying back and forth.

The sensible thing would have been to get up immediately and crouch in a doorway. Instead, we were paralyzed by fear and distrust of our environment. We lay in bed holding tight to each other until the movement subsided.

When a major loss occurs in your life, your sense of reality and security is shaken in a similar fashion. It's hard to get moving, but being paralyzed by fear and distrust isn't going to get you back on balance. You need to believe there is a purpose to all that is happening, and work with it.

I don't mean there is some purpose for your loss. If you believe your loss has happened to teach you some lesson or to punish you, the work of recovery will be more difficult. It is better to accept the fact that some things happen to us and our loved ones for no reason at all. Some things, including tragedies, just happen. This world *is* dependable, and one of the things you can depend on is loss and grief.

One of the most common questions I hear from bereaved persons is, "What have I done wrong? Is this a punishment?" It's certainly an understandable question. But it is also a foolish one for which there is no good answer except "no." Bad things happen to bad people *and* to good people. Loss and grief are not inflicted upon you or anyone else by design. They happen because you are alive in a mortal and imperfect world.

To grow through loss you have to learn that the fact of loss does not diminish life.

Be responsible for your own grief process.

A motto for success used by many super-achievers goes like this: *If it is to be, it is up to me.* That's a great motto for grief recovery, too.

No one can do your grieving for you. No one else can make your decisions or feel your feelings or cry tears that are essential for recovering from major loss. That's one reason it is so important for you to see grief not as an illness from which to recover, but as old-fashioned hard work that you must do.

Throughout the process of your grief work, you will do best if you maintain a personal responsibility for completing it.

The most difficult time to stay responsible for your grief recovery is when depression hits. When sadness is complicated by fatigue, and when things that normally bring joy don't stir you, it is hard to feel responsible for anything.

> No one can do your grieving for you.

Depression is a way of taking time out from working through grief. You might say doing grief work is like lifting a barbell over your head. Perhaps you can lift it once, twice, or ten times. But there comes a time when the weight is too heavy and your muscles are too tired to lift it once more. At that moment you have no choice but to rest your arms before trying to lift it again.

Depression associated with grief can become so intense that you require medication. If it persists, you may need to be hospitalized. But even then, it is finally *you* who must choose to come out of the depression.

Because grief work is so intense, it is important to know when to relax and divert yourself from it occasionally, to help yourself regain strength for the "next round."

Don't quit grief work too soon, however. This is an important point to remember. If you *do* take time out, have a plan ready for getting back to grief work a little later—and then do it!

Don't be afraid to ask for help.

To ask for help is not to give up responsibility for your grief. It means you recognize that lifting yourself up by the shoestrings usually results in a hernia or broken shoestrings—it doesn't lift you off the floor!

Remember one of the key facts about grief recovery: Effective grief work is not done alone. You need others when trying to work your way out of the sadness and depression that follow a major loss.

The sharing that takes place in our weekly grief support group is just part of the group's value. A network of mutual support has developed between sessions that is extremely important. Some "veterans" have made themselves available to the newcomers for emergency telephone calls. We update and distribute a roster of grief-support-group members every few weeks. We put an asterisk next to the names of those people who are willing to be called at any time for support.

The security of knowing somebody is always available who understands grief makes the program work. Sometimes the simplest act counts the most. Two of our older widows were finding their evening dinner to be the loneliest time of the day. Neither of them was eating properly or regularly. One woman drives a car on a limited basis, the other not at all. By mapping out a route that kept them off the busiest streets, I was able to arrange for the one who drives to pick up the other to dine at a local cafeteria on a regular basis. Within two weeks I saw marked improvements in their energy levels and outlooks. Our group meetings are scheduled intentionally to end at 5:00 P.M. More than half of those present go out to dinner together following the meeting. It's a time of laughter and fellowship. It also means that at least once a week they are not eating alone.

You should not be afraid to ask for help. Just as important, the person you ask must understand the grief-recovery process. The best support you can find will come from others who are working through their own losses. You can find such people in every community.

I was a guest speaker at a church one Sunday. The minister announced that I would be available to meet on the following Tuesday with anyone who had experienced a major loss. Fully ten percent of the congregation showed up for the meeting. Experiences like this have taught me that loss and grief are universal experiences. Given an opportunity to share and the promise of an open, accepting atmosphere, many people will respond.

If you look for others who are as eager as you are to work through loss and grief, you will have no trouble finding them. If you can find a leader who is trained in grief and loss, that's a bonus. If you can't, just gather a group and use this book as your guide. You'll find more information about this in Appendix C, which gives you specific guidelines for forming a group and directing the first twelve sessions.

Don't rush it.

I am not known for patience. One of my dear friends, a ninety-two-year-old widow who "adopted" me after the death of her husband, calls me *Reverend Buzz Bomb*. It's a title that causes me to wince only because of its accuracy. I have always believed the best time to accomplish anything was yesterday. I walk fast, talk fast, and eat fast, much to my wife's disdain! I live in the high-speed lane and wouldn't have it any other way. The most difficult thing about writing this book was that there was no way to rush it.

> It will take at least two or three years to work through a death or divorce.

I have much sympathy with those of you who have problems being patient with your grief. However, with all the compassion I can muster, I must tell you this: Grief work can't be rushed. It will take at least two or three years to work through a death or divorce.

Irene worked as hard as anyone I know to get through the death of her husband. She said to me soon after his death, "Bob, I don't intend to let my grief own me. I intend to attack it with everything I've got and to seek all the help I can get. It may take others two or three years, but not me!"

She *did* attack her grief. Irene never tried to avoid any part of it, or any feeling that came with it. She was able to cry openly. She poured herself into helping others in the grief support group. She sought the help of one of the best psychologists in our city. I can't think of one thing Irene could have done that she didn't do.

Nevertheless, when Irene's journey through grief was finished, two years and nine months had passed. The process just can't be rushed. It will take more time than you think you can bear, but you can and you will.

More Things to Do

As part of your grief work, try these exercises. They will help you get closer to your feelings and will give you ways to talk with others about your grief.

After you complete the survey at the beginning of this chapter, share it with at least two others.

Write each of the four statements listed below on a 3-x-5–inch card. Concentrate on one of them each day. On the back of the card, outline what you think the statement means for your grief experience. Share those insights with four different people.

Here are the statements:

- I believe my grief has a purpose and an end.
- I will be responsible for my own grief process.
- I will not be afraid to ask for help.
- I will not try to rush my recovery.

9

Grief and Growth

Growing through loss

You already know that grief is about losing. You need to know that it can also be about growing.

During the first weeks and months after a death, divorce, or any major loss in your life, you will need to be reminded many times that you will not always feel as you do now. You may think the pain of your loss will never go away. It may seem as if the feelings of sadness and emptiness will last forever. You may think you have smiled for the last time in your life. To have these thoughts and feelings is quite normal. The truth is, the pain will diminish, the sadness will leave, and laughter will return.

If you work at it, the grieving process can become a time of growth. The way out of grief may not be a nice, neat stair-climb, but there *is* a way to conquer it. Your path to recovery will have many ups and downs, but if you stay with it, you will emerge stronger than when you started.

Some of the downs you can expect will come after several months, even a year or more. There is no magic time when everything will be okay again. If you know what to expect, you can avoid being harsh on yourself and adding to your own sadness. You don't need to fall into the trap of thinking, "I am the only one who feels this way."

For instance, you may reach a point, perhaps six months after your loss, when you feel better. You will begin to function more normally—

you will sleep better, food will taste better, and you will perform routine tasks as you did before your loss. Days will go along fairly smoothly.

Then something off-the-wall will hit you. You may hear a familiar song on the radio or see a person walking on the street who bears a striking resemblance to your deceased spouse. Perhaps you hear that your divorced mate is about to remarry or that someone has been named to fill your old job.

> Hitting a low just shows how far up you have already been.

Whatever it is, your response is to have the roof cave in on your emotions. When this happens, it is common to think you have slipped and are starting your grieving all over again. That simply isn't true. You are exactly where you should be.

Many people have the same experience. A widow said, "Hitting a low just shows how far up you have already been." They will happen again. They aren't setbacks; they are signs of forward movement. Look at these upsets as mileposts along the way to grief recovery and as signs of personal growth.

I have led grief support groups for twenty-five years. It isn't uncommon to see folks come to the group for the first time eighteen months to two years after the death of a spouse or child. They will say, "I thought I was doing so well until one day I woke up feeling as if I were starting all over again."

When something like that happens, remind yourself that grief is not a bad word. It isn't something you shouldn't feel. There is no particular emotional place you have to be at a given time.

> The inevitable emotional upheavals are surefire signs that you are doing fine.

The inevitable emotional upheavals are surefire signs that you are doing fine. If you continue to face your grief and work your way through your loss, you will come out at the other end a stronger person than you were when you started.

The following exercise is designed to help you see that grief is manageable. It lets you personalize your sense of loss by writing a letter that begins *Dear Grief*. In the letter, you can describe whatever it is you would like to say to your grief, as though you were standing face-to-face.

The exercise continues with a second letter, written twenty-four hours later. This letter is from your grief to you. It describes whatever it is you think your grief is trying to communicate to you.

I have seen marvelous healing and growth begin with this simple act of letter writing. Four months after her husband's death, Irene wrote the following:

> Dear Grief,
> You are a rascal. You take our energy, our organizational abilities, and our brains and do strange things with them. I was prepared for the immediate grief and to feel the loss of my spouse for a long, long time. I was not prepared for the laziness, low energy level, and the stress.
>
> I am impatient with it all. You take so much out of us when we really need to be able to function well. I do not understand why.
>
> I must confess you've done good things for me also. I am more compassionate, understanding, tolerant. You have given me new ways to be of service, and God will show me those ways. Perhaps after I've had more time to look back I will feel different about you, but for right now you are not one of my favorite friends. I am a better person because of you and I must not lose sight of that.
>
> *Sincerely,*
> *Irene*

A day later she wrote this letter to herself from her grief:

> Dear Irene,
> I'm sorry I've caused you so much pain. Remember that your pastor said at the funeral, "Grief is the noblest emotion of all." It truly is the last gift of love you can give your husband, so experience it in a normal way. Let your own time frame happen.

I know you are working hard to get through this phase
of your life. I commend you for that. But I also want to
say, "Let go and let God." Just put it in God's hands. I suggest you read the verses on death in the Bible. Remember,
there is an atomic bomb of hope waiting to explode between the front and back covers of your Bible. I sense
your excitement as you search through those scriptures.
You may be truly amazed at what you find.

Begin to use your time more wisely. Get extra sleep
once or twice a week. You'll be all right. Soon your energy
level will return. You may even lose the weight you've
been trying to lose for some time. In time you will walk
lighter. You will sit lighter. You will feel great.

I am your friend. I am a part of life. There is a purpose
for me. You will see.

Sincerely,
Grief

The attitude Irene expressed toward her grief in those letters was the
key to her return to a full and productive life. She is again a person with
a zest for living and an energy level that sparkles. She is positive, outgoing, and healthy. Irene has successfully handled a terrible loss. She
has also been a great help to dozens of others at times of similar losses.

One Sunday Irene took me by the arm after church and said, "I have
to tell you. It doesn't hurt anymore. I can enjoy the memories of our life
together without having my enjoyment canceled by the pain of losing
him. I am ready to live the rest of my life fully now."

That moment and the shine in Irene's eyes remains one of my all-
time greatest memories. It will be a source of hope whenever my own
next grief experience comes.

Grief is always about losing. People like Irene have taught me that
it can also be about growing and winning. The personal growth Irene
experienced is possible for you too as you work through your losses.

I first began to connect grief and growth when I started meeting regularly with a group of bereaved people. As they talked about the many

facets of their grief experience, I felt some of the incredible depth of sadness that accompanies such losses.

But something else was present, too. I saw those people laugh together at how forgetful one can become under the stress of grief. I saw new skills, talents, and compassion emerge from one person after another. A strong sense of unity developed among those people as they shared experiences with each other. "I didn't know anyone else did that" became a motto for the group.

A widow went back to school and is now enjoying the career she always wanted, but which she put aside for many years to be home with her husband.

> I saw new skills, talents, and compassion emerge from one person after another.

A man who, in his own words, "couldn't successfully boil water," joined a cooking class at a community college after his wife's death. He now prepares gourmet meals for friends.

Several people learned they could do mechanical things they never thought possible before their spouse's death. There was a sense throughout the group that life had put each one to the ultimate test, and each was able to meet it!

Look at the box on this page, which lists some of the ways it is possible to grow through loss. I have never seen this kind of growth happen as a result of winning a lottery, achieving success in business, or

Growing through Loss

This is what it means to grow through loss:

- Growth means gaining a new love and reverence for life.
- It means shifting your attention from the ordinary to the quality elements of life.
- Growth is a greater awareness of our mutual need for each other and of the sacred dimension of life.

reaping a windfall of any kind. I see it weekly in persons who are work-ing their way through loss and grief.

That doesn't mean grief is an experience to be treasured. None of us wants to feel the horrible emptiness and desolation that comes with a major loss. Yet we need to understand that feelings of grief won't hurt us if we face them and work our way through them. Working through loss can also mean growing through loss. The depth of grief hurts, but it can be a cre-ative hurt.

> Working through loss can also mean growing through loss. The depth of grief hurts, but it can be a cre-ative hurt.

When our first grandchild was born, our daughter-in-law and son chose to have her by natural childbirth. They went through training classes and when the time of birth came, he was with her in the deliv-ery room as her coach. We waited outside the door with the other eager grandparents-to-be. Within a few minutes of our granddaughter's ar-rival, we were ushered in to see mother and baby.

Our daughter-in-law's first words were, "I'll never do it again this way, it hurt too much!" An hour later the memory of the pain was just a part of the total experience of creating a new life. By the next day it was something she had met and conquered. They have since had two more children by the same method. That's *creative hurt*.

The pain of grief can also be creative hurt. It is real and long-lasting, but it is not permanent. It passes. Not only does it pass, but it can help create new life along the way—yours.

Help from Others

The most helpful person to a newly widowed person is another widow or widower. When Irene goes to call on a new widow in our church, she has something to offer that I cannot give. Her presence—as one who has sur-vived the experience and come out on top—says in a way that nothing else can

> The most helpful person to a newly widowed person is another widow or widower.

that there is real hope for others. I might say there is hope. Irene has *lived* it.

Over and over, I have seen one widow anticipate the exact day and hour that another widow needs to receive a telephone call and a word of encouragement. It is no coincidence. Once you have been there you understand what is happening, when it happens, and what needs to be done.

Likewise, no one else can listen to someone in the midst of a divorce like the person who has been there and made it through.

"I know how you feel" can be words of comfort or can sound like fingernails across a chalkboard. It all depends on whether the one speaking these words has the experience to back them up. It also requires a sensitive understanding that no one ever really knows exactly how another person is feeling—especially about something as emotionally loaded as a major loss.

> "I know how you feel" can be words of comfort or can sound like fingernails across a chalkboard.

Some years ago, when the aerospace industry went through one of its many cutbacks, several men in our church lost their jobs. They were engineers and lab technicians who were well educated and who performed their jobs with skill. Being unemployed was the last thing on their minds until it happened.

An astute businessman saved the day for many of them. He gathered these men into a sharing-and-support group. There they were free to talk about how terrible it felt to be laid off and how much their sense of self-worth was hurting. They didn't have to be strong with each other as they thought they had to do at home and in church. They gave each other acceptance and encouragement as one after another retrained for a new work field. About two years after it started, the group disbanded because it was no longer needed.

Those men experienced grief as a result of losing their jobs, dreams, and a sense of

> No one could help them through it better than they could help each other.

self-esteem. No one could help them through it better than they could help each other.

My wife, June, responded to a mastectomy because of breast cancer by becoming a volunteer with the American Cancer Society. The program, Reach to Recovery, sends a woman who has had a mastectomy to visit another woman who has just experienced the loss of one or both breasts. The notes and telephone calls that June receives later make it abundantly clear how much it helps. Recently we were sitting in a restaurant when a woman walked up to the table. She pulled June to her feet and embraced her in a big hug. She didn't even look at me as she proudly pulled her shoulders back to let June see the silhouette of her reconstructed breast. She asked if June would meet her new husband and brought him over to the table. Only after several minutes had passed did she look at me and nod a greeting. Before they left, she

Take Inventory of Your Losses

What loss have you had recently? Think back over the past two years.

- When have you had periods of sadness?
- What was happening at those times?
- Make a list of your losses. Read it aloud.
- What feelings do you have as you hear yourself announcing your losses?
- Make a list of your strongest feelings. Read through the list of "feeling words" in Appendix B to express yourself more clearly.
- Have you had occasions when it seemed that other people were critical of or uncaring toward you?
- Have you had any illnesses?
- Are any of your family relationships more stressed than usual?

looked at me again and said, "You have a marvelous wife. I don't know what I would have done without her."

You can decide to grow through the most devastating loss in your life! A major part of the growing side of grief is coming to understand that, in the midst of a life-changing loss, we still have control over our own destiny. You may not be able to choose all of the circumstances of your life, but you can always choose your responses to whatever happens.

I urge you to begin now.

One way to begin is to take inventory of your losses. You might ask yourself the questions in the box on page 102. All the questions refer to what can be considered signs of unresolved grief in your life. All of them are occasions of loss. You can also make them into occasions of growth.

To achieve the happiness you would like for yourself, pay attention to your losses and begin working through your grief. The process takes time to learn and will take a lifetime to do. Fortunately, a lifetime is exactly what we have been given for the task.

10

A Test of Endurance

Life after loss takes time

Of all the challenges you face in working through grief, none is more demanding than the endurance it requires. It begins with 365 days of "the first time without," but it doesn't end there.

If your spouse or child has died, you can't bear to think recovering from that loss is going to take as long as three years. But rarely is it less and often it is much longer.

No newly divorced person wants to think in terms of two or more years before life feels as if it is back on an even keel. It takes all of that time to recover from a lost love if you work hard at the task.

It's tempting for both widowed and divorced persons to try to fill the gap of loneliness by getting involved with another person as soon as possible. You need to know that it often does not result in more happiness, but in greater sadness. You aren't ready for the emotional stress and may not make wise choices. If filling the empty places becomes a substitute for working through your grief, it can also become a detriment to your physical health.

The length of your grief after any major loss will be considerably longer than you expect. It takes a long time to work through the various phases of recovery. To endure the time it takes you must believe the rewards are worth the effort. Trying to rush the process is an exercise in futility—and can lengthen the time required for you to recover your sense of balance.

Grief Is Heavy

Fatigue is one of the most common symptoms of people working through grief. Grief is heavy. Carrying its weight is tiring. People tell me they are constantly exhausted in the first three to six months after a death or divorce.

It isn't that grief beats on you so much as it *leans* on you. In the early months, you feel its weight night and day without relief. It seems to wear you down by persistence.

> People tell me they are constantly exhausted in the first three to six months after a death or divorce.

When Dick lost a business because of an unscrupulous partner, he spent a solid week in bed, too weary to bathe or get dressed. If you are so tired after a major loss that everything you do is an effort, you are reacting in a normal way. It's a heavy load and it takes an incredible amount of endurance to carry it.

The stress of carrying the load of your grief may result in feelings of depression. You may have little interest in eating regularly or paying attention to the nutritional balance of your meals. If you are like most people, you will be dehydrated and you will not get an adequate amount of exercise. You may have trouble sleeping or staying awake.

Fatigue is a normal part of grief recovery. You may want to add this statement to the growing list of helpful reminders you post around your house:

Grief is heavy. To feel tired is normal. My fatigue will not last forever. I will endure until I win.

Grief recovery is hard work that requires a maximum of stamina and patience from you. Whatever else you may call your movement through grief, you will surely label it an endurance contest of the first order.

Your Physical Health

Health problems are much more likely to develop after a major loss. The classic study done by Erich Lindemann in 1944 indicates that one's risk of developing coronary artery disease becomes 250 percent higher after the death of a spouse. Risks for developing cancer, high blood pressure, arthritis, diabetes, thyroid disease, and skin disease are similarly high for those who have suffered the loss of a spouse.

> Fill two one-quart bottles with water and place them where they are easily reached in the front of your refrigerator.

Subsequent studies, including those of Dr. Glen Davidson at Southern Illinois University, indicate an increased risk for migraine headaches, chronic depression, low-back pain, and blood-chemistry disorders. Widows and widowers are also at increased risk for developing alcohol and drug dependency.

The good news is, you do not have to become a victim of health problems. Your response to the grief that follows a major loss is in your control. Take a look at the box on pages 108 to 111 for five helpful ways you can stay strong in the face of grief.

Developing Grief Fitness

Working through grief is a little like working out for physical fitness. Those who lift weights cannot start with the maximum weight they hope to lift. Those who jog or walk can't begin with a maximum distance. They have to work up to these goals a little at a time. In the same way, you don't start out handling grief in the way you will later. You grow into grief fitness a little at a time. It doesn't come easily, but it is the way to regain your balance in life after a major loss.

> You don't start out handling grief in the way you will later. You grow into grief fitness a little at a time.

Over and over you will need to tell yourself, "I will not always feel as I do now." You will need patience with others and with yourself. You will need to remember that sometimes you will feel worse before you begin to feel better.

How to Take Care of Yourself after a Loss

Dr. Glen Davidson recommends taking the following five actions to strengthen yourself for the work of grief recovery. In looking at more than one hundred factors, only these five were found to make a measurable difference in protecting health. The sooner you begin, the better!

1. **Be part of a support group.** Nothing is more important for your physical health than having a group of people to talk to about what you are experiencing.

Where people gather who have all experienced a common loss lies built-in healing power. The single most common complaint I have heard from bereaved persons is the difficulty in finding someone who will listen with compassion to the stories of their losses. Your need to talk about your loss will far exceed the willingness of most family members and friends to listen.

A grief support group does not require highly skilled professional leadership to be effective. Appendix C at the back of this book provides instructions for twelve sessions. This plan has worked successfully for many people, and it will work for you.

continues >

It isn't uncommon during the first year or two to have times when you think the work is finished. And then something happens to plunge you back into the depths of anguish.

The first year after a death or any major loss is dominated by constant reminders. Every day is another *first time without* experience. The more significant the day, the more painful the experience. Birthdays, anniversaries, special family days, religious holidays, and typical vacation dates are among those that are frequently the most painful.

Take things one day at a time, even one experience at a time. It may come down to enduring one more night of loneliness or one more meal across from an empty chair.

2. Drink an adequate amount of water. Under the stress and emotional upheaval of grief, you will tend to be dehydrated without being aware of it. Over the length of time required for recovery, this dehydration can weaken your immune system.

The ideal amount to drink is two quarts of pure water each day. It's a large quantity and, yes, drinking this much does have the expected result on your bladder. But it works! If you just can't get down that much water, do the best you can. One quart isn't as good as two, but it is much better than none.

Fill two one-quart bottles with water and place them where they are easily reached in the front of your refrigerator. If your tap water is not pure, buy bottled water or get a filter. Some people find it helps to add a slice of lemon to the water. The main thing is to consistently drink as much as you can, up to two quarts a day.

Note: Soft drinks (regular or diet), iced tea, coffee, and alcoholic beverages are *not* substitutes for water. In fact, these can work against you, requiring an even greater pure-water intake.

3. Eat nutritiously. While it may be challenging, it is important to maintain a well-balanced nutritional plan while you are

continues >

It helps to know the first year after a major loss is not going to be one of the best years in your life. But it doesn't have to be the worst year, either. After all, it has a purpose and a direction. You can come to the end of the year and know you have made a significant accomplishment just because you survived.

"I didn't think I could do it, but I did."

Passing the anniversary date of a major loss can be like a graduation day. People say to me, "I didn't think I could do it, but I did." I see a new sparkle in their eyes. They have endured the worst and survived. You, too, can do that.

struggling through grief. Avoid junk food; high-fat foods; and excesses of sugar, caffeine, and alcohol.

The challenge for most of us is that eating is a social occasion. If you have to eat alone, food may not interest you during the early weeks and months after a major loss. It is common for people to put off eating until hunger reaches the point of discomfort, then overeat the wrong kinds of foods. The best plan is to try to maintain your weight within five pounds of what it was prior to your loss.

You will find a list of desirable foods and a sample menu in Appendix A of this book. If you have physical problems, check with your doctor for suggested guidelines.

4. Get adequate exercise. Exercise, within the boundaries of your own limitations, is helpful both physically and emotionally. Forty-five minutes of brisk walking does wonders for relieving the symptoms of depression—and it's free! If you have back, knee, or hip problems, walk in a swimming pool. The resistance of the water adds to the value of the exercise and supports your body while you are doing it. Stretching, swimming, and whatever level

continues >

The Lonely Year

The second year of grief calls for more patience with yourself than with anyone else. After getting through the first year, you may think life will return to normal. It doesn't. Many bereaved people call the second year of grief their *lonely year*. They say that surviving the first year proves you will make it. The second year proves how lonely it can be to make it without the one you lost.

It may seem as if you are starting all over again. You aren't. This is a good time to join a grief support group or to rejoin if you dropped out.

of aerobic exercise your doctor permits can all be of great benefit to you.

You will tend to exercise more regularly if you get someone to do it with you. The most difficult part of any exercise program is doing it when you don't feel like doing it. Usually you will feel better and have more energy when you are finished. Having a friend who will help keep you on track to do your exercise is a great help.

5. Get sufficient rest. There is no substitute for getting enough rest while dealing with grief. It is good if you can stay as close as possible to the sleeping pattern you had before your loss. Because of the fatigue and stress involved with grief, it is even better to get additional rest in the form of naps for the first several months after your loss.

Sleep disturbance is very common after any major loss. On pages 184 to 186, you will find instructions for ways to help you stabilize your sleeping patterns. It includes a detailed plan to follow if you wake up in the middle of the night and can't get back to sleep.

Sometimes you will feel worse before you begin to feel better.

Once the second-year crisis is past, you will be ready to start getting on with the reorganization of your life after loss. This doesn't mean there is no more grieving to do. It means you will have developed sufficient skills to handle your grief.

Many bereaved people call the second year of grief their *lonely year*.

In time and with hard work, the good days will begin to outnumber the bad ones.

By the end of the third year, the pain of your loss should be diminished to the point where it finally seems manageable.

By the end of the third year, the pain of your loss should be diminished to the point where it finally seems manageable.

Perhaps the most important growth that will come to you during grief recovery is the sense of confidence and pride that emerges. You have endured the very worst of all experiences and finished on top. You are a different person, a stronger person, and a better person than when you started.

11

Beliefs that Help or Hurt

The use and abuse of religion

Religious beliefs are a vital element in grief recovery. If you are not a person who embraces religion, it makes a difference when a major loss occurs. If you do hold religious beliefs, it makes a difference what you expect from your faith.

People of faith do not have an automatic pass to excuse them from the challenges of grief recovery. It isn't that nonreligious people have a more difficult time and are more susceptible to physical problems than religious people. The fact is that almost everyone has some sort of a belief system that is called into play when a major loss occurs.

My wife and I grew up as people who did not practice religion. Neither of our families attended church when we were children. As we became young adults, we were not antireligion. We simply gave it no thought.

It was two months after our marriage when my wife's young brother was killed. He was playing with another boy in front of his parent's house and ran into the street. A car struck him, stopped, then backed over him. He died a few hours later.

When the news reached us, waves of shock and disbelief rolled over us. The first words out of our nonreligious mouths were, "Oh, God, not Ronnie! Please, don't let it be true."

Like many others, the fact that we never went to church didn't keep the name, "God," from our vocabulary when tragedy struck. We were totally ignorant about the Bible and didn't have a clue what prayer was all about. We just knew we were hurting more than we had ever dreamed possible. We felt helpless in the face of this unthinkable loss. We didn't know where else to turn, so we called out the name of God.

In the months that followed, we blamed God for Ronnie's death. We promised ourselves never to care about anyone so much again because God was so cruel.

We may have been disinterested in spiritual matters before our loss, but when confronted with death and grief, God was at the center of our thoughts.

Our experience is common. Several years later, I became a clergyman. I have officiated at more than a thousand funeral services. Time and time again, I saw people going through the same challenges that we did—and asking the same questions: "Where is God?" "How could God let this happen?"

It isn't any easier for people of faith when they experience a major loss. In fact, people of faith often ask exactly the same questions as everybody else at such times.

Talking about God and religion in times of major loss is almost universal.

- "I lost my faith in God when my husband died of cancer."
- "How can God allow such a thing to happen to an innocent child?"
- "Why did God take my loved one from me?"
- "My faith is all that held me together when we divorced."
- "Knowing my child is with God gives me the courage to go on."
- "My church was there for me and my family. I will always be grateful."

These statements all come from people who experienced a major loss. Every one of them expresses a normal reaction when life comes crashing down in a heap. Each of them expresses some form of religious faith.

The important issue for grief recovery is whether any belief system has a positive or a negative impact.

Spiritual beliefs can help you cope with major losses. They can work for you as you make your way through the process of grief and recover a sense of joy in your life.

Your beliefs can also be an almost insurmountable barrier to healing the deep wounds that have been inflicted upon you.

It all depends upon what you believe and how you practice your beliefs.

Dr. Howard Clinebell Jr., an internationally recognized authority on grief and loss, says a healthy religious faith and the support of a spiritual community have a unique ability to help turn *miserable minuses* into *positive pluses*. He affirms that religion can provide incredible strength for the task of grief recovery.

In her book, *Living through Personal Crisis*, Ann Kaiser Stearns says, "Faith is a powerful energy when it represents the trust that, with struggle, our sorrows can be overcome."[1]

However, religious faith can also get in the way of recovery.

"Make-a-Wish" religion is very popular. It is the kind of religious expression you see on some television programs. It's very "me"-centered. It assumes that the sphere of prayer is something like sitting on Santa's lap with a wish-list for Christmas. If you are good enough, your wish will be granted—and you will avoid the human losses experienced by the rest of the world.

This inappropriate, unhealthy religion looks for short, simple answers to complex questions for which there are no simple answers. It hopes for some magical way to either bypass grief or to resolve it quickly and painlessly.

If you look upon religious faith as an inoculation against the kinds of tragedies that happen to others, you will be unprepared when you experience a major loss—as you surely will. Faith in God is not a quick fix for sorrow and mourning. A reasonable expectation for healing the emotional wounds of grief is two to three years at the least. You will not handle your grief more easily because you are a religious person.

The requirements for healthy grief recovery are exactly the same for believers as for nonbelievers.

"Make-a-Wish" religion ignores one of the basic facts of human life: **This is a mortal, frail, imperfect world in which the word *fair* doesn't always apply.**

Anna was the mother of two sons, both in their early forties. "Her boys" were the center of her life after her husband died suddenly from a heart attack. Anna could not believe her ears when she received a telephone call saying that one of her sons had taken his own life. The wounds from this terrible loss left a gaping hole in her life that was not even beginning to heal a year later—when her other son also committed suicide.

When Anna joined our grief support group, all of us wept with her as she related the horror of her story. She had tried going to a church group in another city to find comfort for her pain. Instead, she was told that suicide was a sin and her boys were doomed for eternity. She felt the unspoken question was, "What had she done to deserve such sorrow?" The pastor made it abundantly clear that all of her losses were God's will to test her character and faith.

There was nothing fair about Anna's losses. There certainly was nothing fair or helpful in the response of that church and its pastor. Her grief wounds could have been deep, unresolved, and, perhaps, fatal if she had not rebelled against that kind of hurtful religion.

Anna's subsequent return to a good and satisfying life started with her understanding that this is, after all, a mortal, frail, imperfect world in which the word *fair* doesn't always apply. That understanding enabled her to move beyond the "Why?" questions and begin building a new life for herself.

When our daughter, Jeanne, was in high school, we lived in a small community. There was a tightly knit sense of unity between the students, teachers, and parents.

Jeanne was one of seven song leaders who performed at sporting events and parades. During her senior year, one of the other song leaders was killed in an accident. She was riding with her boyfriend in an open vehicle on a mountain road. In a moment of carelessness, he lost control and the vehicle rolled, throwing out Jan and crushing her. She died instantly.

The funeral, held in the local mortuary, was packed with grieving students, parents, teachers, and community leaders. Everyone was in a state of shock. As we arrived, we passed small groups of teenagers huddled together, sobbing uncontrollably as they tried vainly to console each other. Again and again, I heard young voices asking why God would allow a tragedy like this to happen.

As the service started, more than two hundred pairs of tear-filled young eyes looked hopefully at the minister who was leading the funeral. When he began his sermon, I started to feel sick in the pit of my stomach.

He told those grief-stricken people that Jan's death was a blessing. He said God was out walking in the heavenly garden, looking for the most beautiful flower to pick. Jan was chosen. He praised the young man whose mistake had caused her death for having such faith that he could smile and praise God that Jan was in heaven.

I wanted to stand up and scream, "NO!" I probably would have made matters worse if it hadn't been for my more-in-control wife. She placed her hand on top of my white knuckles, gripping the seat in front of me, and quietly said, "Not now. It isn't the time." She was right. I hope this book is the right time at last.

Some of those young people left that place thinking they should not be too good, or they might be next on God's flower list. Others were encouraged to bury their grief and anger where it could fester and grow. Jan's boyfriend went on "praising the Lord" until the day he collapsed and wound up hospitalized to have extensive psychiatric treatment. Years later, I learned that at least seventy-five of those two hundred teenagers eventually required professional psychological treatment of some kind.

This experience and that of Anna remain for me the classic examples of the abuse of religion as a resource for grief recovery.

Letting Go of "Why?" Questions

Yearning for some rational explanation of tragic events is as normal as breathing. Asking "why" after a major loss is a common part of the grief recovery process, but it represents just one step along the way to wholeness. Recovery depends upon, among other things, letting go of the "why?" questions and turning to questions that begin with words such as "how" and "what." "How do I go on with my life now that this has happened?" and "What can I do to recover a sense of joy and meaning in my life?"

> Whatever our religious orientation, the message is the same: Experiencing major losses, even though painful beyond words, is not optional.

Questions beginning with "how?" or "what?" imply an acknowledgment of the loss and an affirmation of survival.

When we experience a major loss, the only answer to the question "why?" is that this is a mortal, frail, imperfect world in which the word *fair* doesn't always apply. The world is not perfect and life does not follow a perfect script. This is a world that operates by the laws of gravity and physics. Therefore, accidents do happen. It is a world in which human beings have free will. Therefore, mistakes will be made and cruel, violent acts will take place.

We live near Tempe, Arizona, a high-energy, rapidly growing college town with a festive atmosphere. A young, single mother moved to Tempe from Chicago to get away from the dangers of her inner-city neighborhood. A month after she arrived, she stepped outside her apartment, holding her baby in her arms. A shot rang out, and she fell to the ground, mortally wounded. A deranged neighbor didn't like the music she had been playing, and he shot her.

Trying to explain the "why?" of such an event is as foolish as it is meaningless.

Whatever our religious orientation, the message is the same: Experiencing major losses, even though painful beyond words, is not optional. There is no grand plan or purpose to every loss we face. There is neither a divine nor a demonic plot to "get us." It's just part of living in this less-than-perfect world.

Beliefs That Help

Dell and Liz were active laypersons in their church. They held leadership positions that gave both of them high visibility. Both were equally well known in the community. People thought of them as the ideal married couple, warm and caring. When they announced they were getting a divorce, it came as a total shock to all who knew them.

Both of them felt that they were not only failing at marriage and as parents, but they were also betraying their church and friends. The church they belonged to was a large one and, at first, they made an effort to both remain in the congregation. It seemed possible that they could coexist with the many programs and multiple worship services, but it was not to be.

Dell transferred his membership to another church and soon was involved in the leadership of that church. Liz remained in her church where she organized a singles program that became a major tool for support and for church growth.

During the stress and conflict of their divorce proceedings, neither Dell nor Liz blamed God for their struggles. Both expressed strong faith in God's acceptance and found their hope for new lives among the people of their churches.

In time, both have remarried and gone on to happy and fulfilling lives.

Out of one couple's very real grief experience has emerged help and encouragement for others. Liz also developed a new career that has brought her much satisfaction. Both remain positive forces in their community.

Dell and Liz's faith was able to encompass something as challenging as divorce. The congregation was willing to enter into their loss and grieve with them without being judgmental. Because everyone involved practiced a healthy religious faith, something very good came out of a painful loss.

Four Ways Religion Helps

There are four very distinct, precise ways that a healthy religious faith, used appropriately, can be of tremendous help at a time of major loss.

1. Religion influences one's fundamental view of life.

There are two fundamentally different points of view from which to begin the task of grief recovery: For the nonbeliever, life is temporary and death is permanent. For the believer, death is temporary and life is permanent. These statements represent vastly different starting points for the task of grief recovery. The task to be done is the same for both, but the underlying belief system is quite different.

For the nonbeliever, death is the great *canceled* stamp on every achievement. One may have achieved many good things in life, but all that is canceled by death. To see life as temporary and death as permanent is to live by the motto, "It was nice while it lasted, but it's all over now."

The permanency of death gives greater power to all the other losses in life. A beer advertisement proclaims, "You only go around once in life, so grab for all the gusto you can." The implication is we must get it now because there is no tomorrow. So, what if I invest all my life in a career—and am laid off? What if the marriage I meant to last forever ends in divorce? How do I face the inevitable decline in my physical strength that comes with age? How do I begin the process of grieving for my lost loved one?

I know there are answers for nonbelieving people because I see them recover from major losses. I must admit, however, that I don't know what those answers are.

For believers, the starting point of grief recovery is different. Death is not seen as the great cancellation. Death is no more than the ultimate nuisance in life. I believe life is permanent and death is temporary. This does not in any way diminish the pain I feel when a loved one dies, nor does it make major losses any less real.

The believer looks at the experience of grieving as a dark valley through which to walk, just as the nonbeliever does. But for the believer the dark valley is not a box canyon. It is something through which to travel to get to a destination on the other side.

Death can wreak havoc in our lives, but according to my faith system, neither death nor any other major loss has the power to cancel anything. I said that to a group of single parents and was asked, "What about divorce?" One lady said, "Those who lose their husbands to death are lucky. They can go to a grave and express their mourning and pray for the deceased. In my case, he is still walking around after our divorce and I only wish he were dead!" But even that woman had to admit that not all of her marriage had been bad. There had been moments of intimacy and times that were wonderful. The divorce did not have the power to cancel out those experiences unless she allowed it to.

I meet with a large number of people every week in a grief support group. Most are widowed, a few are divorced, some have lost children, and a few have spouses with Alzheimer's disease. These folks are able to express deep love and sentiment for their loved ones, even years after the person's death. They are able to relive precious moments and shed tears freely as we talk about the life they shared together. The dominant emotion, through tears and all, is that of joy. They know it isn't over—it's just interrupted.

2. Religious faith can provide the motivation required for grief recovery.

Recovery from grief takes a long time. Grief is fatiguing. It wears you down. Indescribable anguish can rip and tear at your insides, making the smallest responsibilities seem overwhelming. Sometimes just remembering a name or your telephone number is impossible.

Even while anguish pummels your feelings to the point of numbness, an oppressive, silent sadness leans on you, too, without ever seeming to let up. Under this kind of pressure, we need to be motivated to take the first steps toward recovery. The first step on the path to renewed joy and vitality after a major loss is the most difficult of all.

> The first step on the path to renewed joy and vitality after a major loss is the most difficult of all.

This is the point at which a grief support group can be so important, but often taking that step is extremely difficult. Here, religious faith can play a major role and supply that motivation.

Jewish and Christian scriptures provide vivid images to help motivate us enough to take at least a baby step on the long road to recovery. The most familiar image is that found in the Psalms: "Yea, though I walk through the valley of the shadow of death, I will fear no evil." It is powerful imagery. It affirms that somebody has done it before. Nearly all newly bereaved people think they are the only ones to feel as they do. It also says that the path of grief is not a dead-end street but a well-marked trail leading to a destination.

3. *Religion is a great antidote for the loneliness that accompanies every major loss.*

One factor of grief that is common to all, regardless of the kind of loss experienced, is loneliness.

- "I am the only one who has ever felt this way."
- "Nobody else can understand my grief."
- "I am alone and I will always feel as I do right now."

To eat alone, watch a sunset alone, see some historic event on television alone, or just have a passing thought with no one else with whom to share it can cause fresh pain in each instance. The single most common complaint among widowed persons is, "My need to talk to someone about my loss far exceeds the willingness of my family and friends to listen to me."

Those in the Christian tradition tell me there is great comfort in the words attributed to Jesus at the close of the Gospel of Matthew: "Remember, I am with you until the end of the age." I would interpret those words to mean loneliness is always an illusion. The statement means that *even if everyone else deserts me, I am not alone.* That belief has held me together more than once in a time of personal loss. It doesn't make the pain of our losses any less, but it can make them bearable.

4. Your religious community can provide supportive strength.

Never underestimate the supportive power of a religious community (church, synagogue, or fellowship). For all the failings of people in our churches and synagogues, there are no other groups who do so much at a time of major loss.

Funerals or memorial services held in the familiar surroundings of the bereaved person's regular place of worship offer a warmth not found in mortuary chapels. The simple act of providing food and a reception following the service—or taking food to the home—brings a sense of belonging and the assurance of being loved.

Ministers, priests, and rabbis are the only professionally trained persons in our society who do not need an invitation to reach out to people at a time of any major loss. Many times someone in our congregation has asked me to visit a neighbor or friend who has lost a loved one to death or who has gone through a divorce. In most cases, these are not people who have attended our church. They did not call to request my involvement, they just shared their sorrow with a neighbor or friend. I have never been refused entrance to a home when I have called. A doctor cannot do that and neither can a psychologist nor social worker. It is a rare privilege given to religious leaders, and with the privilege comes responsibility.

For all the religious community does, so much more can be done. Traditionally, congregations have been directly involved in supportive ways with bereaved people for about one week. With all that we now know about the length of a normal grief recovery, it is imperative that congregations be involved for a minimum of three years. No other group in society is in such an advantageous position to be with people for the long haul. Providing grief support groups and divorce recovery groups, making contact on the anniversary of a death, and providing one-on-one contact to make reentry into church worship and activities easier are all ways that churches and synagogues help people through grief.

In some churches, a minister or layperson delivers a plant or flower arrangement to widowed persons on the anniversary of their spouse's death. Placing a silk rose in a green plant carries the message that the congregation hasn't forgotten and continues to care.

Survivors are often challenged by a household responsibility that was carried out by the one who is now deceased. There are churches that keep a list of persons with skills in the most common areas of expertise, such as accounting, plumbing, electricity, automotive maintenance, cooking, and driving a car. When someone makes a need like this known, the church is able to refer the call to a volunteer, who provides the requested assistance.

Other churches have provided "shepherds" or other caregivers who are available to initiate contact on a regular basis to offer a listening ear. This has proven especially helpful to divorcing persons as well as to those who have lost a spouse or child to death.

In all of these ways, a healthy religious faith and a sensitive religious community can be of tremendous help in a time of major loss.

Three Things Religion Cannot Do

There are only three things that religious faith cannot do for us. Understanding and accepting these limitations is as important for grief recovery as using the things that faith does so well.

1. Religious faith cannot grant us immunity from loss.

Practicing "fire insurance" religion (reading the Bible, attending services, tithing, praying, and doing good deeds for the primary purpose of avoiding divine "punishment") leaves folks ill-prepared to cope with the losses that are an inherent part of being a real person in this mortal world. Being persons of faith does not excuse us from our own mortality or that of our loved ones.

> It's vitally important to understand that death, divorce, and other major losses are not necessarily deserved or the result of God taking time out from looking after us.

Those who pretend that the rules of life are different for people of faith face an almost certain sense of guilt when something goes wrong. We hear this point of view in such statements as, "I wonder what he (or she) did to deserve that?" or, "Somebody up there was sure looking out for you this time." I hear bereaved survivors question how God could allow their loved one to die when he or she "was such a good person who was loved so much."

It's vitally important to understand that death, divorce, and other major losses are not necessarily deserved or the result of God taking time out from looking after us. The rain falls on the good and not-so-good alike. Good fortune seems to pour out on people without much regard to their morals or religious character—and so do major losses.

In the early days of our religious experience, my wife and I belonged to a prayer group. We not only met to pray for ourselves, but also to pray for and visit sick people in their homes or in the hospital. A request came for the group to pray for a woman who was diagnosed with inoperable cancer. A tumor in her abdomen was the size of a grapefruit. She was given no chance for survival. Three members of the prayer group went to her home and prayed for her.

Upon her next visit to the doctor, the examination showed the tumor was gone. Needless to say there was joyful celebration, not only in her household, but also among members of the prayer group. They were sure God had intervened in response to their prayers and faithfulness. A month later, the woman died of a heart attack.

More recently, my wife and I were driving to a meeting at 2:30 P.M. on a clear, sunny Sunday afternoon. As we approached an intersection, the light turned green for us, and all cross-traffic was stopped. The intersection was empty. As we slowed, then proceeded through, we never saw the car that ran the red light and hit us broadside. Police estimated it was traveling at least forty-five miles per hour at impact. Our car was totaled, but we escaped with only moderate injuries.

The response of some church members was, "This can't happen to you—we can't get along without you." Others said, "God was sure looking out for you." A few days later, four teenagers were killed when their car went out of control and hit a light pole only a few blocks from the scene of our accident.

If we survived our accident because God was looking out for us, does that mean God decided not to care about those young people? If the woman whom the prayer group prayed for recovered from cancer because of their prayers, does it mean they failed to pray adequately for her heart? Or does God "draw straws" to see when we win or lose?

It seems to me to make much more sense, and to be much more in harmony with the basic tenets of the Judeo-Christian heritage, to say, "This is a mortal, imperfect, frail, and flawed world. Life is not always fair. Tragedy and major loss are as much a part of life as victory and times of joy. As a human being, I am subject to these realities. So are my loved ones. My one and only assurance from God is that I will never be deserted in any circumstance."

Such a perspective may not be comfortable, but it is real, and it provides a solid foundation for using faith in the most helpful way at the time of a major loss.

2. Religious faith cannot give us back our dead loved ones or our dead relationships.

The one thing bereaved persons want more than anything else is to have their loved ones returned to them. It is the one thing that neither God nor we can give them.

> Strange as it may seem, to acknowledge this fact up front with a survivor is always comforting.

Strange as it may seem, to acknowledge this fact up front with a survivor is always comforting. It says that we understand the enormity of the loss, and it lets the bereaved person know that we have no simple or pat answers. In the face of a major loss, every person needs compassion, understanding, a listening ear, and people who are willing to carry out needed tasks without being asked. To downplay the pain of a death or divorce with religious platitudes frequently only magnifies the sense of loss.

For the caregiver to acknowledge the finality of the loss is often the beginning of the journey to recovery for the survivor. Loss means gone forever, at least for the duration of this life. The mechanism of denial is overcome when the survivor understands *and acts on* this excruciatingly painful reality. It is at this point that the most basic decision of recovery can be made: "I will live." That pledge will have to be renewed many times throughout the first year of recovery.

To acknowledge that our religious faith cannot bring back our dead loved ones is in no way a denial of life after death. I have no doubt that my friends and family members who have died are "okay" in God's eternal heaven. While that affirmation gives me a certain sense of comfort *for them*, it does not diminish my sadness or loneliness at losing them. Whatever else their condition is, one thing is clear: I will not see them again in this life. That part of my history is ended.

Frequently people are told that their loved ones are in a better place and they will one day be reunited. When this kind of thing is said in a way that implies the bereaved person's grief should therefore be lessened, it becomes very hurtful. It can even inhibit grief recovery and increase the health risk of the bereaved person.

We must understand that "loss" equals "gone and gone forever." The possibility for a full and rewarding life after any loss begins with this understanding.

3. Religious faith cannot provide a shortcut through grief.

Every clergyperson I know wishes this were not true. We would give anything to find a pathway of faith that would take people from the point of their losses to a full recovery—and do it quickly. Unfortunately, such a shortcut isn't available to us.

It is another of those strange-but-true facts of grief recovery that religious faith serves us best when we

> "We want you to know we will be with you every step of the way."

start out understanding that the pain of grief will not be less nor will the path to recovery be shorter because of our religion.

Again, for the sake of the physical health of bereaved persons if nothing else, clergy and laity must never let people think that because they have prayed for them, the bereaved's grief should be lessened. People who maintain a classic "stiff upper lip" and who come back to church without tears should not be publicly praised or held up as the ideal of faith. More often than not, those who are having the worst time—who weep uncontrollably and seem to need the most help—are actually doing the best job of grieving.

Trying to shortcut the grieving process is like giving someone with hypoglycemia a major dose of sugar. The person might feel quite high—for a little while—but an even greater crash will follow.

The divorcing and the bereaved need assurance from their pastors and congregations that their church will not desert them over the long haul of grief recovery. The church can provide support groups, special programs dealing with losses, and a bereavement-care team, and it can make the effort to *maintain* contact with those who have suffered a major loss for at least two years (three is better). In these ways the church can say, "We know this is a long, tough, and painful journey for you. We want you to know we will be with you every step of the way."

Religion and You

Religion and the religious community can be tremendous resources for you in times of major loss. But understand that loss and grief are a part of life for the believer and nonbeliever alike. All of us are subject to disappointment, heartbreak, and death. When we suffer a major loss it hurts—regardless of our faith or lack of faith.

> When we suffer a major loss it hurts—regardless of our faith or lack of faith.

You will search for hope. The kind of hope that will serve you best acknowledges life will never be the same again, but insists that life after loss can still be full and good. The resources of religious faith can be strong motivators to reach for this hope. If you believe God has been present with human losses for a long time, you will be encouraged to try again when you want to quit. You will be able to accept new places, new stages of life. You will know that whatever challenges you face now, or in some future loss, you will not face them alone.

12

Quiet Losses

Private struggles grieved in silence

This chapter written with June Deits.

JUNE:

All losses are worthy of grief. There is no such thing as an easy loss. If it doesn't hurt, it isn't a loss. You have already read in this book that the worst kind of a loss is the one that happens to you.

However, the pain of a loss can be even more intense if you perceive that you can't talk about it. Experts call such losses *disenfranchised*. I prefer to call them *quiet losses*. There are no sounds heard by the world around as you make your way through the dark valley of grief. The pain is excruciating, as with all major losses, but seems magnified because you think it must be kept to yourself. With quiet losses, there aren't any arms to reach out and hold you, or sympathetic shoulders on which to cry. The dominant word in your head is *shame*.

Throughout this book, Bob has been sharing real-life stories of real people, while carefully protecting their identities with fictitious names. As we talked about this chapter on silent losses, we considered hiding my identity. However, precisely because these "quiet losses" are usually suffered alone, we decided not to do that. Therefore, instead of Bob writing about my experiences and covering my identity, I will tell you about them personally.

When I look back at my childhood, I see a little person wrapped up in a blanket of guilt and fear. There are few photographs of me as a young child in which I am smiling. Outwardly, I appeared to be a very independent, if overly serious, child. No one seemed to notice that I cried when I heard music and bit my fingernails until they bled. I think no one noticed because I would not allow anyone to get close to me, emotionally or physically.

The Loss of Innocence

It was just after my fourth birthday when I was the victim of sexual abuse for the first time. Without a vocabulary to describe it or any understanding of the magnitude of the loss, my childhood innocence about sexuality was taken from me. For almost fifty years I didn't talk about it because the pain and the fear were too great. Somehow, I buried the events below the level of my conscious mind. I "forgot" it ever happened—but it was with me every day.

One day, out of the blue, the memories started coming back. The images were terrifying and disgusting. I had to decide if I could tell anyone, including my husband. It was not an easy decision. But I knew if I kept it to myself any longer, it would destroy me.

Those of you reading this book who have been victims of abuse will understand. There are many of you. Studies indicate up to fifty percent of women and forty percent of men have been the victims of some form of sexual abuse as children. This means there are millions of us who have suffered in silence. In doing so, we make one of the most difficult experiences in life more painful than it already is.

It's my hope that as I break the silence and talk about my experience, it will help you to face your own past without fear. Perhaps you, too, can cease being quiet about your loss.

I was barely four when a neighbor became a friend to my parents. I'm sure they never suspected that his real motive was getting access to me. When "the mister," as I was told to call him, first offered to swing me on his backyard play set, I was thrilled. It was great to have the attention of this grandfatherly man. Soon, however, I came to dread our visits to his home. He would take me into a storage shed, hold me on his lap so I couldn't move, and warn me not to yell or I would be in trouble with my parents. His hands were rough and caused intense pain in places on my body I barely understood. If I cried, he told me that it was my fault that it hurt.

There were many such occasions, but to this day I don't know how many. I just remember the frequent nightmares that grew more frightening all the time. In time, we moved to another neighborhood and the visits to "the mister" stopped. There was no more physical pain, and I was left with no outward marks on my body. However, the emotional scars ran much deeper—and have never completely gone away.

My body had become sexualized long before its time. The innocence of childhood was gone. As I grew, there always seemed to be a vulnerability about me that invited unwanted advances from male playmates and other grown men. I blamed myself and wondered what I had done to deserve it. My farm-raised father once commented that I attracted men like an animal in heat. I was less than eight years old at the time.

I pushed it all deep inside and tried not to remember.

When Bob and I were married the day after my nineteenth birthday, I wasn't thinking about "the mister." Bob and I had not had sex before our marriage (although the idea crossed our minds every time we were alone). Once the vows were said, I thought my suffering would be at an end. I was wrong.

From the beginning, I struggled with our sexual relationship, allowing myself no more than moments of pleasure. If Bob walked up behind me and simply put his arms around me, I froze. I couldn't explain it to him because I didn't know why I did it either. I continued to chew my nails and dread any intrusion into my private space.

For all that was good in my life, including a husband who loved me, three precious children, and a large circle of friends, I was never content inside. I often wondered why memories of my childhood were always sad. I blamed myself for my discontent and my struggles with sex.

During the year of my fifty-first birthday, all that was bottled up inside came to the surface. The memories of going to "the mister's" house flashed into consciousness and then disappeared into the darkness again. The first time it happened, I was driving alone in our car on a busy city street. I began shaking all over, and my eyes were blinded with tears. I pulled to the side of the road to avoid having an accident and sat there, trying to decide if I were going crazy. I was frightened, confused, and filled with anger. I hoped the images would go away and never come back again. They did go away—for a few days. Then, they came back, again and again until they would not go away at all.

The challenge was working up the courage to tell Bob. We have always been very close with no secrets from each other. Bob is my best friend. Nevertheless, this one was tough to share.

I hesitantly told Bob about the flashbacks. Just breaking the awful silence of forty-seven years was its own reward. As my memories unfolded, I told him everything. The tears he shed with me for the innocence lost by a little girl became a healing balm for me and for a wounded little child who still lives inside me.

The more we talked, the more I was able to see that it wasn't my fault. He helped me to see that I had done nothing wrong. I learned that many children bury hurtful memories. With the silence finally broken, I discovered I was a normal person who was now ready to deal with a terrible experience in a healthy way.

Contentment didn't come over night, but it came. The final step in putting the past to rest was standing before a thousand people in our church and sharing my story with them. I have subsequently repeated it in workshops and seminars across the country. The response is always the same. Women and men shake my hand or give me a hug and whisper in my ear that they too are victims of childhood sexual abuse. They thank me for opening the door to their memories or giving them the courage to begin talking about their experiences. Some tell me that it was while they were listening to me that they faced their own experience for the first time. On one occasion, Bob and I spoke to seventy-five military chaplains. At their request, I shared my story. Ten women chaplains and two men sought me out afterward to let me know we shared a common secret. I urged them to form a support group with each other so they could have a safe place to break the silence.

No Longer Silent

The loss of innocence is a terrible loss. I don't know if it hurts worse than losing your spouse, or a child, but I do know the pain is excruciating. Those whose minds cannot cope with the emotional pain often do what I did: bury it below the level of consciousness. If that meant that it had gone away, it would be okay, but it isn't gone, and it surely isn't okay.

This hidden emotional wound diminished the quality of my adolescent and adult life. I could not explain my nervousness. I was ashamed that I could not keep from biting my fingernails. I was sure Bob was disappointed in my on-again, off-again sexual desires. The pain of childbirth seemed like the punishment I deserved for something I could not describe. There never was a time when I felt totally contented or happy.

It was only when I broke the silence barrier that my healing began. It is difficult to put my sense of relief into words. Over the ensuing years, I have walked more lightly and laughed more easily than ever before in my life.

It was essential for my own growth and healing to release the anger I felt toward "the mister" and my parents. As I talked about it, I realized that he was an old man with a twisted personality, and my parents were too unsophisticated to know how to deal with it. My father's sense of ethics would mean either he would actually have to shoot the man or move his family away. He did the latter, not out of cowardice, but out of compassion for us.

My value as a person is not diminished by the tragedy of my experience. I am not less desirable as a woman or a wife. My life is good—very good.

But first the silence had to be broken.

If you are reading this with more than a detached interest, my thoughts are with you. You start by facing the experience head-on. It often helps to put your memories and feelings in writing. Find at least one trustworthy person with whom you can share everything. Write yourself reminders that you did nothing wrong and nothing of your value as a person has been taken from you.

Here are some of my discoveries:

- As you break the silence, you will find your pain decreasing.
- If you listen carefully, you will find others who are also suffering in silence. You can find more healing together than any of you will find alone.
- Find a way to let go of your stored up anger. It's hurting you far more than those at whom it is aimed.
- Don't be afraid to enjoy your first feelings of relief and joy. You deserve them.

Loss of Body Parts

The loss of innocence is not the only loss that is difficult to share with others.

On Valentine's Day, 1994, I lost my left breast to cancer. Until that time, I never considered how much the loss of a body part impacts emotions—or how difficult it is to talk about it.

My awareness of the problem changed the day my routine mammogram revealed a suspicious cluster of calcifications. This time, there was no question about Bob's awareness. He heard the news at the same time I did. He was also on the telephone when the doctor called to say the biopsy had revealed cancer.

Once the initial shock and disbelief subsided, we realized we had to make two decisions:

1. What kind of treatment should I have?
2. Who do we tell about this frightening development?

Telling our grown children was automatic. The challenge was to decide who else should hear about it. Bob was the senior minister of a church where attendance sometimes exceeds 2,000. Because of the earlier editions of *Life after Loss*, we lecture and lead seminars across the nation. We are in contact with thousands of people who know us and care about us. I wondered just how private or public I should be with the news of my cancer.

One part of me wanted to keep the news secret. I could have whatever surgical procedure was required, and no one but Bob would know the difference. We could make up a story about why I needed a little time off from public activity. No one outside my family would have to know that the symbol of my femininity had been disfigured. If I were fortunate enough to overcome the cancer, they would never know at all.

Cancer seemed like a "dirty" disease to me. I was aware that people who smoke or eat high-fat diets are at higher risk for cancer. I could just hear the whispers, "What has she done to get cancer?" I felt bad enough on my own because I thought my body had betrayed me.

If I had broken a bone, contracted a virus of some kind, or even had a coronary problem, I would not have had the same desire for secrecy. They seem like "clean" problems, even though they can be as life threatening as cancer.

However, I had cancer, and I had to deal with it and with my desire to keep silent about it.

I learned very quickly that the only sensible treatment for me was the complete removal of my breast. Because the mammogram had discovered it early, the cancer was not invasive. There was no spreading of the cancer to lymph nodes or other parts of my body. I was, therefore, a candidate for an implant. This positive news actually reinforced my option for silence. My body would not be disfigured, at least outwardly. Nobody would know except those I chose to tell.

Bob and I talked at great lengths in the days between my diagnosis and my surgery. I knew he would not think less of me with only one breast, but I wondered if I would be as sexually desirable as before. Bob assured me he would feel no differently. He reminded me that the primary purpose of the female breast is to nurse children. Since those days were decades into the past, he wondered how many more babies I planned to nurse. It helped to put the challenge in a new perspective.

He also assured me that he wanted whatever option gave me the best chance to survive.

I have never been obsessed with the appearance of my body. I had thyroid surgery when I was a young woman. There has always been a faint scar across my throat since that time. It never bothered me. I have "stretch marks" on my abdomen as the legacy for giving birth to three children. Giving up a breast, I discovered, was quite another challenge.

I think it is the connection between breasts or other parts of the body related to sexuality that makes it especially challenging to lose them. It also makes it more difficult to talk about it.

It wasn't just my physical attractiveness to Bob that I thought might change. My own sense of identity as a woman was involved. My breast was more than an appendage on my body. It was part of who I am as a feminine person.

Letting it go was not easy—until I weighed the value of my life against a breast. Whatever emotions of sadness I would have at its loss, at least I would be alive to have them.

I wrote a personal letter headed, "Good-bye, My Breast." I thanked my breast for being part of me for so many years and for the beauty it had brought to my body. I expressed gratitude for its function when babies were born and for the pleasure of feeling my lover touch it. I assured my breast that although an artificial mound would replace it for cosmetic purposes, nothing would ever take its place in my heart.

I knew it was time to break the silence once more.

If I was struggling with the challenge of cancer and losing a breast, so were others who were also struggling in silence. They deserved to have someone open the door to talking about it. I determined to be one who would do it.

On the Sunday before my surgery, Bob informed the whole church that I had breast cancer and would have a mastectomy. Following the service, I stood with him at the back door as people were leaving.

One woman after another stepped up, took my hand, and said, "I am a ten-year survivor," "I am a twenty-year survivor," "I am trying to decide what to do myself." Men shared with me that they had been victims of prostate cancer, wished me well, and reminded me that life is more precious than any part of the body or any body function. To my great surprise, it was the men who were, if anything, most supportive and encouraging.

I would be less than honest if I didn't acknowledge that there were some men and women who did not respond in helpful ways. Some people made an obvious point of shaking Bob's hand, but walking around me as if I either was not there or breast cancer was contagious. Others touched me as if I was suddenly breakable. Several glanced in the direction of my chest, as if to see which breast was affected. Several of my friends just didn't want to talk about it. Women with whom I had shared in-depth conversations in the past now wanted no more than a minute to pass the time of day.

Such reactions were to be expected. I knew that. I could have been guilty of similar forms of rejection with other women in the past and never have known it. But rejections were a tiny minority. The vast majority of people with whom I shared the news of my cancer were very supportive.

On the day of my mastectomy the prayers of more than 2,000 people were with me.

As soon as I was recovered sufficiently from the mastectomy, I formed a cancer support group for women. We met in one room while Bob met with the husbands or boyfriends of the women in his office. We have mourned the death of two of our members. It was comforting to know they did not have to die in silence.

I became a volunteer in the American Cancer Society program called Reach to Recovery. I visit other women just before or after breast cancer surgery. In addition to delivering a packet of helpful materials, often including a temporary prosthesis, I am an agent of listening and encouragement. It is another way to help break the silence barrier.

Bob took me with him when he visited people in the church prior to their cancer surgeries of any kind. They are glad to have him come and pray with them, but he says they really want him out of the way as soon as possible so they can talk to a cancer survivor.

We started an annual "Daffodil Sunday" in our church. Daffodils are the official flower of the American Cancer Society, the first flower of spring and a sign of hope. People make donations that go to cancer research in return for daffodils placed on the altar in honor or memory of someone who is a cancer survivor or who has died from cancer. A list of those names is printed in the bulletin. During the service, people in the congregation who are cancer survivors are invited to stand, if they are comfortable doing so. More than a thousand have used this means to break the silence of their own cancers in the past five years. We also had raised in excess of $60,000 for cancer research as this book was being prepared.

Bob and I make presentations on the subject of "Coping with Cancer as a Couple." It has opened the door for many others to break the bonds of their silence.

All this has come about because I made the decision not to keep my cancer a private matter. In some ways, it has felt as if I were making private parts of my body visible to the whole world. I wish I could turn the clock back and not have had cancer at all. Every time I look in a mirror at my chest that has one breast and one "mound," I wish I still had two normal breasts. Nevertheless, I discovered there is life after the loss of a breast—or any body part. There is an end to grieving that loss. Healing comes as much from refusing to be quiet about it as from the defeat of the illness.

To keep silence is like having a wound that never completely heals. We have known people who lived with colostomies or artificial limbs who did everything they could to keep their "handicaps" secret. There have been women who had breasts or uteruses removed and men who lost sexual function due to prostate surgery. Bob knew of a few men who had testicles removed. I can only imagine the fears and shame of these people because none of them ever talked about it.

BOB:

Other Quiet Losses

People with AIDS are often looked upon as the modern equivalent of the biblical leper. Sam and Mary always prepared communion for their church. It was a task they loved. Their son was diagnosed with AIDS and came home to be with them while he was getting treatment. Sam and Mary were afraid if the people in the church discovered their dark secret, they would not want them touching the communion materials. They went in to see their minister and hesitantly told him of their predicament. The temptation was high to try to keep the situation secret. The minister realized there could be no support for Sam and Mary if no one knew about their tragedy. Together, they decided to tell the church leaders. Sam and Mary offered to resign. Their offer was rejected, and they were surrounded with love and prayers through their son's illness and subsequent death. It was a terrible ordeal for Sam, Mary, and their son, but it would have been infinitely worse if they remained quiet.

I know a mother whose only children were two sons. They both told her they were gay on the same day. She never could talk about it openly and agonized in silence because her dreams of grandchildren would never be realized.

The death of a pet can bring grief that is difficult to share for fear of looking weak or foolish. Well-meaning friends who suggest "get another one and get over it" don't help.

We have known people who moved from one state to another as a result of a job promotion. The deep grief they felt at leaving familiar places and people was masked behind smiling faces. They privately ask, "Who will understand my sadness when I should be so happy?"

Not everybody will understand. That's a simple fact of this real world. If you don't expect everybody to react sympathetically, you won't add to your disappointments. You can be sure that many more will support you than reject you. Be sure you focus your attention on those who give support. Don't take your cues from people who don't understand your sadness.

I found the following exercise to be helpful. Try it. I think you will like it.

1. Identify a loss that is difficult for you to talk about.
2. Write down what you think would happen if other people knew about it. Read it out loud to yourself at least three times. Do you need to change anything?

3. Find someone with whom you can risk sharing your experience and ask them to read what you have written. Talk about your feelings.
4. Ask that person to help you identify the possible positive outcome of letting others know what has happened to you. How might other people actually be helped?
5. Choose the most appealing of these and experiment in pursuing that outcome.

Read the balance of this book and follow the guidance it gives for recovering from any loss—especially the quiet ones.

13

Children and Grief

It's a big hurt for little people, too

Try to imagine what it is like to experience the death of a loved one, the breakup of your family, or any other major loss as a child. If you can imagine these circumstances, you have some idea of how children grieve:

- You have all the sadness, fear, anger, and other emotions that adults have.
- You do not have the vocabulary to express the way you are feeling.
- Your limited exposure to life leaves you with little understanding of what is happening to you.
- You probably assume you are to blame in some way.

When someone dies, children feel the loss as much as any adult. They just don't have the words to tell us about their feelings.

Remember that while adults internalize their feelings, children act them out. Their vocabulary may be limited, but their behavior can reveal volumes about their feelings.

When adults try to shelter and protect them from the experience, children turn to their own imaginations, which often suggest a situation even worse than the real one. Young children often assume they are somehow to blame for the loss. They are used to thinking in terms

Young children often assume they are somehow to blame for the loss.

of blame for spilled drinks and broken toys. It's easy for children to interpret the combination of adult silence and sadness as disappointment in *them*. If a parent or grandparent dies, the child may think that all adults in his or her life will die. If parents divorce, children may think it is they who are no longer loved.

As adults, we play a crucial role in the future lives of children after they experience a major loss. When the adults respond in ways that help the child face loss and work through grief just as we must do, there are no lasting emotional scars. When adults fail to respond in helpful ways, the effects may be seen for the rest of the child's life. Among these effects is the continuation of the problem to another generation. The child who carries grief wounds into adulthood will tend to be uncaring and unhelpful to others in times of grief.

Remember: While adults internalize feelings, children act them out.

Matthew and Lisa were six and eight years old respectively when their mother put them in the kitchen with bowls of cereal, went into the family den, and shot herself. The children found her body and called neighbors for help.

The children's father was wise enough to take them to a skilled counselor. She sat on the floor with Matthew and Lisa, helping them draw pictures of their mommy. Some of their pictures reflected their child's anger at mom for leaving them. Others showed the fear they were feeling. Others depicted better times when mom was happy.

On the day of the funeral, Matthew and Lisa placed some of their drawings in the casket with the body of their mother. Each child added a small gift they had chosen.

Over the next several months, the counselor helped them understand that their mother did not die because she was angry at them. She assured them her death had nothing to do with their failure to pick up clothes or toys. It wasn't because they had been naughty or hadn't eaten everything on their plates at dinner. Mom was very sad down inside. She loved them and didn't mean to make them sad. Her death was a tragic event that she couldn't help.

Sunday school teachers in Matthew and Lisa's church were instructed to be prepared to listen to them carefully and to be sure they understood it was not God's will for their mother to die.

In time, their father remarried. Matthew and Lisa have become happy in their new home. They have come to love their stepmother, who has made sure they have pleasant memories of their biological mother. Now, several years later, they are contented, well-adjusted children. The wounds of the past have healed.

> When the adults respond in ways that help the child face loss and work through grief just as we must do, there are no lasting emotional scars.

When the adults in a child's life do not respond in appropriate ways, the results can be drastically different than Matthew and Lisa's experience.

Rosemary was about the same age as Matthew and Lisa when her life was turned upside down. Her father, who suffered from chronic depression, was successful in taking his own life on the fourth attempt. Unfortunately for Rosemary, the adults in her life did not respond in a healthy way as happened with Matthew and Lisa.

Her mother became addicted to alcohol and drugs; withdrew from the support of family, friends, and church; and "went off the deep end." She entered into multiple sexual relationships and worked only sporadically. Rosemary reverted to bedwetting, lost weight, and couldn't sleep. She seemed frightened and insecure. The probability is high that Rosemary has suffered emotional scars that will damage the quality of her life for a long time to come.

Telling Children about Death

To provide the opportunity for healing that children need after a death, adults can do the following five things:

1. Provide an open, honest atmosphere in which it is easy for children to ask questions and express their thoughts and feelings. This includes involving children in family discussions about the person, the death, and funeral plans. It may be important to sit on the floor while talking with younger children. Holding them on your lap and giving frequent assurances of their security and your love for them can ease many fears. Remember: While adults internalize feelings, children act them out. Watch for signs that tell you the children need your attention.

2. Understand how children are interpreting their experience with death. I find that asking children specific questions enables them to tell me what they are thinking and feeling. I ask such questions as:

- Have you ever been to a funeral? What was it like?
- Have you ever seen or touched a dead person?
- What do you think you will see at the funeral?
- What else do you know about death and funerals?
- What would you like to know?
- What would you like to ask _____ (name of the deceased person)?

The fact that you are willing to talk matter-of-factly about these things is reassuring to children. It is helpful for you to sit on the floor or at a low table with them. It also helps to provide paper and crayons, a coloring book, or modeling clay to enable children to express themselves nonverbally.

3. Give correct and factual information as simply as you can. Dispel myths and the creations of the child's imagination. Do not use phrases such as "Grandpa has gone away," "Mommy is sleeping" or "God wanted him." Younger children take your words as literal, absolute fact. Children may interpret the statement that a loved one has "gone away" to mean that the deceased person wanted to leave them. If you say the person is "sleeping," they will wait for him or her to wake up. I have heard more than one child say fearfully that "if God wanted this person, God may want me next."

A useful and helpful statement to a young child (under the age of seven) would be something like this:

When someone dies, it means their body is no longer working. Their heart stops beating and they don't breathe anymore. They don't have to eat or sleep. They are never too cold or too hot. Nothing hurts. They don't need their body anymore and that means we won't see them.

This statement has to be repeated many times on subsequent occasions because young children do not perceive death to be a permanent condition.

When her twelve-year-old brother was killed, Dawn, aged three, alternately understood that he was gone and expected to see him again. Michael's body was cremated and taken by the family to another state for burial. Dawn saw ashes in an ashtray at the airport and thought it was Michael. When the plane began its descent, Dawn began to cry, thinking the plane would land on Michael. When they disembarked, she was disappointed he wasn't there to meet them.

Each time the child expresses confusion, you need to repeat the same statement in the same way. Begin by saying, "Remember _____ (name) has died, and when someone dies, it means. . . . "

4. Help children preview what will happen at a viewing, memorial, or funeral service. Describe the physical setting and what the child will see. If possible, show the child a picture of a casket. Describe what the body will look like. If any marks or wounds will be visible, describe them as simply as you can.

One of the most frequently asked questions is, "Should children be allowed to touch the body of the deceased?" The answer is yes, if they want to and if they are prepared for it ahead of time. Children are naturally curious. How something feels is one way they determine if it is safe for them. Try to describe the feel of the body in terms the child can understand. Tell them the person will feel cool instead of warm. Have the child touch your arm and compare the feeling to touching the arm of a vinyl or leather-covered chair. A typical statement to make would go something like this:

You may touch (name) if you want to. However, now that his (or her) body is no longer working, it will feel different. Instead of being warm and soft, it will feel cool and sort of hard. It won't hurt (name) if you touch him (or her) and it won't hurt you.

You may have heard horror stories about children having severe emotional damage done by touching or kissing a dead body. I have never encountered such a reaction, nor has anyone else in my acquaintance who works with death and loss. Such fears seem to reflect more of an adult anxiety about death. The key to all children's experience with death rests with the reaction and response of the adults around them.

5. Provide some means for children to say good-bye. The easiest and one of the most effective ways to do this is to have the children draw a picture that can be placed in the casket. Be sure to make a copy for the child to keep. If children are old enough, they can write notes that are also placed in the casket. Other useful expressions are photographs, especially of the child with the deceased person, cassette-taped messages, toys, or articles of clothing.

It is perfectly okay for children to see adults in tears. Just explain that you miss the deceased person, too, and feel very sad.

Age Makes a Difference

Children grieve and express their sadness in varying ways according to their age and development. It is not that young children do not grieve, they just perceive death and loss differently than adults or older children, and they respond differently. From infancy on, loss and grief are a normal part of human life.

Infancy

Infants show an understanding of loss well before their first birthday. They require physical touch and stroking for their development. Their two basic fears are loud noises and falling. Each of these is associated with a separation from the source of their security.

The first game many babies respond to is peek-a-boo. Interestingly enough, the name comes from Old English and means "alive or dead."

First eye contact is made with the child, then some object is used to block the infant's view. Momentarily, the adult is gone as far as the infant is concerned. Then the object is removed and eye contact is reestablished accompanied by the words, "peek-a-boo." Frequently this contact is reinforced by some physical touch.

A great moment comes in the life of every parent and grandparent when the infant is able to control the game by controlling the object that breaks the eye contact.

Preschool

Through approximately age four, children sense loss and sadness but cannot conceptualize death.

The fear of separation begins at about the age of one. After a death in the family, it is not uncommon for children to be afraid to be away from home or out of their parent's sight.

However, death does not seem permanent. It is more like taking a nap and waking up. The concept of time is limited. It may seem to a young child that death is only being "less alive." With the exposure of most young children to many hours of television, this understanding is reinforced by seeing cartoon characters in particular "dead" on one program and alive on another one that follows.

Anita was four when her grandfather died. When she and her parents arrived at her grandparents' house, her grandfather's body was laid out in a casket in the front room. Anita was told that she must stay in the dining room. She peeked around the corner and saw a room full of adults standing around her grandfather's body. Several were crying because he was dead, but she didn't know what that meant. She wanted him to get up and play with her, but again was told she must stay in the other room.

On the day of the funeral, Anita was not allowed to attend the funeral but was taken to the cemetery. When the casket lid was closed and it was lowered into the ground, she began to cry. She couldn't understand why they were all leaving grandpa alone in the ground. She thought he would be lonely and cold in the dark. She wondered if he had been bad and somebody was mad at him. When it was time to leave, she tried to tell her parents that her grandfather had not kissed her good-bye, but nobody was paying any attention.

Anita still carried the memory of this sad experience when she became a grandmother herself.

Elementary School

Between the ages of five and nine, the understanding of death becomes clear to most children. They come to realize that pets and people die and that death is final.

Jasmine had just celebrated her fifth birthday. She and her ten-year-old brother, Karl, were at home with their father while their mother was at work. The two children were ready for school and their father went out to start the car to take them there. When Jasmine emerged from the house, her father was slumped over the wheel. She ran back inside to tell Karl that daddy was taking a nap in the car. Karl knew something was wrong and called a neighbor for help.

Jasmine ran from person to person, wanting to know when her daddy would take them to school. Karl retreated to his room, knowing their father was dead but not knowing how to tell his sister the bad news.

At the funeral, Jasmine watched her father's body intently. At one point, she tugged on the sleeve of my wife's dress and said, "I think I saw my daddy move. He's waking up now." June replied in a soft voice, "No, Jasmine, your father did not move. He is not sleeping, he is dead." Jasmine leaned against her, took June's hand, and nodded in agreement. "Daddy's dead," she said.

Karl responded to his father's death in much the same way as the adult members of the family. His greatest worries were who would take care of them and would he have to leave school and go to work. Fortunately, Karl had adults around him who were willing to listen and to assure him that everything would work out in time.

Adolescence

By the time a child approaches adolescence, he or she has come a long way from the days of playing peek-a-boo. Death now has a social dimension in which concerns about the consequences are paramount. The death of the same-sex parent when the child is about twelve or thirteen years old seems to have the potential for lasting problems. It is wise to seek professional intervention when possible.

General Guidelines for Talking with Children about Death

The most important insight adults can communicate to children of any age is that life goes on after a death, divorce, or any major loss. To do this, you must become more comfortable with your own grief. The many exercises in this book can help you.

In addressing the needs of children of all ages at a time of loss, you will serve them well if you

- Offer your acceptance of their feelings and behavior.
- Listen carefully without being judgmental.
- Assure them of their security in terms they can understand.
- Make sure they understand they are not to blame. Express your love and care for them in unmistakable ways.
- Act in ways that elicit the children's trust.
- Answer all questions as honestly as you can.
- Help them understand that circumstances will not always be like this and they will not always feel as they do now.
- Provide an atmosphere of stability in the midst of any changes.

As adolescents move further into their teenage years, death raises philosophical questions about the meaning of life. It is a time when they feel immortal and death represents an intrusion of reality that can be terribly painful. If one of their peers dies, it represents a special challenge to their sense of security. If that death happened to be the result of suicide, professional intervention is mandatory. Adolescents often become quite moody after a death, sometimes subjecting themselves to greater risks and impulsive behavior. Inviting teenagers to a grief support group or forming one just for them is quite appropriate.

14

Losses in Later Life

Tarnish on the golden years

A young man said, "When you get older, losses hurt less. Right?" I answered, "Wrong!"

Because of this common, faulty perception, older people have been denied the support and understanding everyone at every age needs when a major loss occurs.

Family and friends make the assumption that older people are more philosophical about death and other losses, and therefore it doesn't hurt as much. The theory goes something like this: *Older people don't expect a spouse or siblings to live forever or to remain physically strong and independent indefinitely. They know that nobody lives forever. They know they have to make adjustments in lifestyle as the impact of age hits them. Therefore, loss doesn't hurt as much as when you are younger.*

It's a great theory, except it has no basis in fact.

People married fifty, sixty, or more years almost breathe in sync. When one of them dies, the survivor's entire basis for making sense out of life is gone. Men expect their wives to outlive them. If she dies first, he often thinks he's done something wrong. If anything, it is worse when a child dies before a parent. *"This is not the way it is supposed to be. My child should be attending my funeral, not me attending my child's funeral."* That's a lament I have heard many, many times.

Widowed men and women in their seventies and eighties miss sexual intimacy as much as anyone else. They just don't talk about it because they think people will laugh at them—and it happens.

Loneliness, for many older people, is the most challenging and long-lasting result of a major loss. Ruby is a delightful, energetic eighty year old, whose husband died seventeen years ago. She is active in her church and has many friends. Outwardly, she appears to have no problems with her life as a widow. Ruby told me she does have a good life, for which she is very thankful. But she also said, "Night time is the worst because it's then that the loneliness overwhelms me."

> "This is not the way it is supposed to be. My child should be attending my funeral, not me attending my child's funeral."

Older adults have fewer options for coping with loneliness than younger people. Some no longer drive a car, and many of those who do cannot see well enough to drive at night. Watching television and reading are the primary forms of escape from loneliness. However, even these activities don't always work. Married couples grow accustomed to talking about everything. A major part of their enjoyment of any event is sharing it with each other. Ann said, "I will be watching a good program on television and instinctively turn to Hal to say, 'wasn't that great?'—and realize he is no longer there." The same kind of thing happens when an old favorite piece of music plays on the radio, or there is a beautiful sunset. It is in these moments that the full impact of loss is felt and the loneliness feels like a crushing weight.

I have known many older couples who helped each other keep going and remain independent as they grew more frail with age. Getting groceries, going to the doctor, or just getting out of the house was only possible by confronting the challenge together. When either of them died, the other not only lost a spouse but also the ability to live independently. For most older people, the word *hell* is spelled, "Nursing home." The disdain felt is so strong I've never been quite sure whether the onset of dementia is a cause or a result of facing life in even the best of such facilities.

Elmer lost his wife to cancer at the age of eighty-three. They had been married fifty-seven years. He had cared for her at home for as long as he could. When she entered a hospice facility, he was there seven days a week. After her death, it became necessary for Elmer to move to an assisted living apartment. It was a beautiful place that offered endless activities and excellent meals. A few weeks after moving in, Elmer came to see me. He was noticeably upset and fighting back tears. When my office door was closed, he hesitantly confessed that he was missing his shop and all his tools as much as he was missing his wife. His marriage and his shop work had defined the meaning of his life since his retirement. Now, both of these major segments of Elmer's life were gone. The pain he was experiencing was as great as anyone's at any age after a major loss.

Earlier versus Later Losses

The process through grief is basically the same at every age. The concepts and exercises you are reading about in this book are equally applicable across the span of a lifetime.

There is really only one major difference between losses in earlier life and losses in later life. Losses in earlier life are usually *accidental*. Losses in later life are usually *incidental*—they go with the territory.

Children and young adults do die of cancer, heart disease, or diabetes, but it isn't the norm. Deaths among younger people are more likely to come from accidents or violent crime. Whatever the cause of death might be, during younger years it has an accidental quality to it.

It can be argued that no divorce is an accident. That's only partly true. People do not get married with the intent of it being a temporary arrangement. Every bride and groom whom I have known intended to be married just once and have it last for a lifetime. Rarely, if ever, does someone set out deliberately to undermine a marriage. In that sense, even divorce can be an accident.

Whatever the loss, if you are under fifty years of age, it seems like a big mistake that somebody should be able to rectify. It's an accident that causes permanent change. However, there is more time to adjust to the changes and to create a new life after any loss.

Among older adults, cancer, heart disease, and numerous other potentially fatal ailments happen frequently enough to be called normal. When senior citizens say, "After sixty, it is patch, patch, patch," they are speaking from experience.

The following charts show the ever-increasing "loss curve" faced by people in later life.

Losses in Later Life

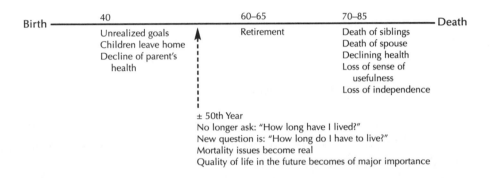

In a typical family, parents are in their forties or fifties when their children begin leaving home. The dynamics are about the same whether parents are still married to each other or are divorced. The family structure of the past eighteen to twenty years is gone. Parents may outwardly seem to celebrate their new freedom, but it is still a loss—and can be a major one. This is also the era when careers are at their peak and the realization comes that some goals are not going to be reached. Parents may experience the death of their own parents during the same period of time. I was thirty when both of my parents died. My wife lost her parents when she was past fifty. The deaths of my parents fall into the "accidental" category. June's father was a victim of

Alzheimer's disease at seventy-seven, and her mother died at eighty-three. The deaths of her parents were "incidental" to growing older.

Somewhere around our fiftieth year, we quit asking, "How long have I lived?" We now ask, "How long do I have to live?" This change in questioning, whether verbal or internal, represents a major change in perception. At this point, the question of our own mortality and that of our loved ones is no longer hypothetical but rather visceral. Quality of life issues rise to the forefront of our thinking. We are concerned with longevity, but we are more concerned with the quality of our lives, however long we live.

There is, of course, the all-important matter of attitude, whatever your chronological age might be. Attitude can impact your health, fitness, and quality of life at any age, but its importance grows as you grow older.

Consider these questions:

1. How old are you?
2. Do you think of yourself as "old?"

Don't be too quick in answering either question. It's not as easy as you might think.

I know people in their thirties who look, act, and think old. I also know people in their seventies, eighties, and nineties whose lifestyle is anything but old.

Al is seventy-nine. He is physically fit and strong, with a physique that many men half his age would like to have. He has been one of the best roller skate dance teachers in the United States for several decades. He's still agile and skilled on skates, teaching even the most difficult dances for hours at a time. Al is not old by anyone's definition.

Imagine that you did not know the date of your birth and you did not have a mirror. How old would you be? The answer is, you would be as old as you perceive yourself to be.

If you say, "I am as old as I feel," then the question is: "On what day?" Personally, some days I feel quite young, whereas on other days I feel older than dirt.

The truth is, we do know the date of our births. And for some strange, self-punishing reason, we look at ourselves in the mirror the first thing every morning. We can't kid ourselves with illusions. Nevertheless, perceptions are still vital.

June and I became great-grandparents in the same year we celebrated our fiftieth wedding anniversary. I also retired the same year. A year later our oldest child reached his fiftieth birthday. A year earlier we had the fiftieth reunion of our high school graduation class—complete with name tags showing our senior class photos. These factors tend to do away with any illusions I have about being young.

However, we dance the Argentine tango with enough skill to perform in public, can dance on roller skates for two hours at a time and ride mountain bikes fifteen to twenty miles a day. On a good day I can still hit a golf ball 250 yards. Sitting remains my least favorite thing to do. As I consider these activities, I don't meet my image of what it is to be old.

My perception is that although I am not old, there is no doubt I am getting older.

Accepting this fact tells me that while I can continue doing many things, I can expect more losses in my life, with greater frequency, as time goes on. My losses will not mean that I am either unlucky or that I'm being picked on. They just go with the territory of later years into which I am moving. Understanding this helps me keep from making my losses worse than they are. It also motivates me to enjoy the moment, not to take myself too seriously, and to stay as active as I can.

Make a list of the facts of your life. Head one column "old" and another "young" or "not-so-old." Check your perspective to see how old you are, regardless of your birth date.

Factors of Normal Aging

I once shared leadership of a conference on aging with a physician who specializes in geriatric medicine. As she spoke about the factors of normal aging, it seemed almost eerie that such information was passed on so calmly. Every factor she listed raised another challenge about getting older. These are some of the *normal* aspects of aging:

- Reflexes slow down.
- Nerve function decreases.
- Muscles become more fibrous and less elastic.
- Vision declines—as does endurance.
- Memory acuteness and speed of comprehension lessen.
- Bones begin to lose fat pads—resulting in pain.
- Lungs don't function as efficiently.
- Food takes longer to digest, causing more intestinal problems.
- The protective coating in the gut decreases and dries out, leading to more problems with constipation.
- The colon tends to "droop."
- Skin gets spots and other blemishes.
- Hair turns gray and often thins.
- Body temperatures are not controlled as well—feeling uncomfortable is more common.
- Color perception changes, making it difficult to coordinate colors appropriately.
- Coordination declines.
- Sleep disturbance is more common.
- Sexual functions are inhibited by other body changes, such as dryness and decreased blood flow.

These are all considered normal factors of aging!

Every one of them represents a personal loss over which we have little or no control. Each of these losses has a negative impact on our sense of self-worth. A diminishing of self-worth is like a magnifying glass on any other major loss that we experience, including the death of a loved one, loss of independence, or relocation.

All of this is unique to losses experienced in later life.

A very dear, sweet lady of eighty-seven years said in a very matter-of-fact way, "Living past eighty is not for sissies." I take her words as the sound wisdom of one who has walked that walk and speaks the truth.

Dr. Andrew Weil said in a lecture, "Aging isn't a disease. Rather, it's a natural breakdown in the efficiency of the body's normal maintenance and repair processes. Aging is simply living past our warranties."

Victim or Survivor?

> Living past eighty is not for sissies.

Coping with losses in later life is another place where the most important decision we can make is to be a survivor, not a victim.

As it is with most losses, the circumstances present themselves without asking our permission. There is no question about avoiding losses associated with later life—we can't. But we can choose the attitude we will take toward those losses and the manner in which we will respond to them.

Choosing to be a victim means being passive and feeling helpless to do anything about the loss.

Choosing to be a survivor means being assertive and realistic without giving up hope. Survivors take responsibility for their own futures. They face their challenges head-on.

Victims ask "Why is this happening to me?"

Survivors ask "How can I get the most out of life, regardless of the circumstances?"

Victims are dominated by fears, doubts, and frustration. They tend to be bitter and negative about life.

Survivors also have fears, doubts, and frustration—but they are determined to conquer them. They tend to be positive and upbeat about life. They give in to the factors of normal aging very begrudgingly. One man who was having increasing problems with joint pain was on the golf course when he said, "I can sit at home and feel pain, or be out doing the things I like to do and have pain. I'm not giving in as long as I can walk!"

Frank was a retired minister with a long history of heart problems. When his wife died, his family decided he should move into an assisted living facility. He was very sad about leaving the house he had shared with his wife for many years. His grief was compounded when he was forced to give up driving a car. Nevertheless, in a matter of weeks, he had become a voluntary chaplain to the other residents, visiting those who were alone and leading a weekly Bible study and worship service.

Losses come to everyone. In later life, they come more frequently. We can't avoid these normal factors of simply getting older.

We can avoid allowing the facts of later life to overcome us. We will have losses, but that doesn't mean we have to be losers!

> We will have losses, but that doesn't mean we have to be losers!

Getting older and experiencing the normal losses of later life cannot be avoided—unless you die young. You can choose to be a survivor instead of a victim.

A very energetic senior citizen said, "My one goal is to not stop living twenty years before I die." It's a worthy goal for all of us.

15

Making New Discoveries

Beginning with loss—ending with life

It's great to talk with people who have made their way through grief! Those who have experienced a major loss and recovered from it remind me of explorers and adventurers.

Have you ever talked with a mountain climber or skydiver? Those who have conquered grief sound like people who have done such exciting and dangerous things. They will tell you not so much about what they have lost as about what they have *discovered*. Their lives will not be lived just in memories of the past, but also in new plans for the future.

If you have had a major loss recently, you probably can't imagine yourself thinking of anything else for the rest of your life. I assure you if you work through your grief in the ways I have been describing, you will not only think of new things, in time you will also sound like an adventurer.

Jean was a young wife with a two-year-old child. Her husband died suddenly after open-heart surgery. For the next three years Jean worked hard at her grief. She was a regular participant in our grief support group. Jean learned stress-reduction techniques and sought counseling for a nutrition plan to strengthen her body for the task. At every step along the way of her recovery, she refused to take the easy way out. In the midst of her own struggles she became one of our most dependable volunteers to visit newly bereaved people.

As she looks back now, Jean would tell you the experience has taught her she can do much more than she ever dreamed she could before Joe's death. Her family verifies she is indeed more confident and self-assured. She recently purchased a brightly colored hot-air balloon and is working toward her pilot's license, a dramatic symbol of the new life she has discovered after a terrible loss.

Jean would gladly give up her new self in exchange for having Joe back. But because getting her husband back is not possible, Jean is building a good life for her daughter and herself. She continues to discover brighter hopes with each new day.

Whereas Jean was a very outgoing person from the beginning, Alice was quiet and shy. She was a contented homemaker and mother of two sons until her husband got cancer. After his death, Alice went through a dark and dismal time that lasted for almost two years. Like Jean, she refused to give in to her grief or to run from it. Alice is convinced that the Kleenex company must have added an extra shift of workers to keep up with her need for tissues!

Today, three years after her loss, she works as a doctor's receptionist. She meets people easily, is considerably more forceful, and dresses in brighter, bolder colors. Alice says, "It's hard to admit I'm a better person today, because it sounds like I'm glad Larry died. Nothing could be further from the truth. I'd give anything to have him back. But I do like the me that is emerging as a result of getting through my grief. I look back and I just can't believe I really did it."

Linda's best friend, Joan, was diagnosed with terminal cancer. Though Linda lived in another state, she quit her job and moved near Joan to lend support to her and her husband, Leonard. Joan's slow death was terribly difficult on both Leonard and Linda. Each of them tried to lend support to the other after she died. Linda felt that a part of her had died with Joan. She had fantasies of being able to take Joan's place in death and allowing her friend to go on with life. Her depression became deep enough that she sought the aid of a psychiatrist.

Her one remaining contact with Joan was the relationship she had with Leonard, who seemed to understand her grief better than anyone else. Three years after Joan's death, Leonard presented her with a gold bracelet on Valentine's Day—and a kiss. It took another year of psychotherapy for Linda to get past her feelings of betraying her deceased friend by falling in love with Leonard. I had the privilege of performing their marriage ceremony.

Making Discoveries

Grief begins with a terrible and painful loss, but it can end with the discovery of new life. For all that is said in a negative way about grief, there is a positive side, too, if you will work through grief.

Jean, Alice, and Linda each discovered a strength of character within themselves they had never known before. Each emerged with a new sense of pride and self-confidence. Each knows she was put to the ultimate test in life and was equal to the challenge. None of them ever wants to experience a major loss again, but all of them know deep inside that if it should happen, they can handle it. This discovery alone has added a new dimension of happiness and security to their lives.

> Grief is not only a door-closer. Grief is also a door-opener.

You can make the same discovery. I believe each of us has a great deal more character than we think. But it often takes some major event in our lives to bring out that character.

Grief is not only a door-closer. Grief is also a door-opener. It's true that you cannot get back a loved one who has died or a part of your body lost to surgery. You aren't likely to get back a marriage that ended in divorce or a dream that was broken. It is equally true, however, that life can still be good for you. Once you have faced your grief squarely and taken the necessary steps to get directly through the center of it, you will see new sources of happiness that you couldn't see before.

When my father and mother died, I made a discovery that has continued to enrich my life from that time on. *I learned how to cry!* Before their deaths I had always handled my sorrow with stoic reserve. In working through my grief following

> Tension and stress that were formerly stored in my neck and back were released through tears.

their loss, I found I was actually healthier because I could cry. Tension and stress that were formerly stored in my neck and back were released through tears. My wife says I became a better husband. My children had a better father; my church, a better minister. In the ensuing years I have discovered that because I am free to cry, I am comfortable with the tears of others. This freedom has opened many new doors to helpful counseling. But I didn't learn the effectiveness of tears in a textbook. I learned it in the laboratory of my own loss and grief, and by allowing myself to be immersed in the grief experiences of others.

Attitude and Expectations Are Important

As uncomfortable as the thought may be, one grief experience does not give you immunity from future losses.

Dan and Dora had two sons. Their younger son died from a virus that caused an inflammation in his brain. Shortly after his death they moved, hoping the new environment would help them adjust to their loss. Sometime later, a daughter was born. Their surviving son, Michael, was twelve years old when he was kidnapped, sexually assaulted, and brutally murdered. In the course of six years, these parents lost two of their three children.

Dan and Dora have taught me many priceless lessons about courage in the face of overwhelming grief. They, like Jean and Alice, did not try to sidestep the impact of their second tragedy. In the early going after Michael's death, they faced their grief under the bright light of media exposure.

Because Michael's body was abandoned in the desert, they were unable to see him after the tragedy. To experience the reality of what had happened, they asked the police to show them pictures taken at the murder scene. Later, they visited the site where it happened.

Pictures of Michael were left up in their home. Conversations about him were carried on daily. Because of local publicity,

They did not expect to be immune from tragedy.

the man who killed their son was put on trial in another city two hundred miles away. When the trial began, Dan and Dora were there. Throughout the trial and afterward, they handled themselves with such openness and poise that they became inspirations to the entire community. A few months after Michael's death, a little girl in our city was abducted and killed. Among the first people to call the parents were Dan and Dora.

Dan and Dora taught me an important lesson, which was that working through the death of Kevin, their first son, helped prepare them for facing Michael's death. The most fundamental aspect of this preparation was they did not expect to be immune from tragedy.

Fortunately, not many of us have to face the kinds of tragedies Dan and Dora faced. But all of us need to remember that the very worst kind of loss is always *ours*.

If we expect to suffer for the rest of our lives after the death of a loved one, it will be difficult to let go and move on to new life. However, if we understand that the effective use of time will get us through grief, we have a foundation for starting the work and beginning the process.

What you expect to discover after any loss plays an important role in your recovery from grief. Your attitude toward the new possibilities that emerge for you is equally important.

What Can Hinder Recovery

I often hear misguided statements like the ones that follow. The attitudes and expectations they represent are like stones blocking the doorway to new discoveries.

- You never recover from a major loss such as death.
- Time is the only healer for grief.
- If you love someone too much, your grief will be worse.
- Nobody else can help you with your grief.
- The death of a spouse is more painful than divorce.

- A slow death is easier to handle than a sudden death.
- Your loss was God's will and you should not question it.
- If you just keep busy, your grief will go away.

Not one of these statements is true! Confronting loss and grief is one area of life where popular opinion is worth less than nothing. To build a new life after loss, you must understand the facts of loss even better than you understand the realities of life.

Statements that reflect significant truths about the experience of loss *do* exist. I have collected some of the most significant ones in the box below.

True Statements about Loss and Grief

The following are true statements. They represent important attitudes and expectations about loss and grief.

- You can recover a full life after a major loss of any kind.
- It takes time to be healed from grief, and it also takes lots of hard work.
- The better your relationship with one who has died, the more satisfying your grief work will be.
- Many people can help you work through your loss, especially others who have had similar losses.

continues >

- Grief that results from divorce is similar in many ways to grief resulting from death and is different in other ways. It is every bit as painful.

- It is never God's will for you to suffer nor for your loved ones to suffer or die. Death and loss are a part of this mortal life.

- If you keep too busy to face your feelings and avoid talking about them, you subject yourself to a higher risk of illness following a major loss.

Viewing loss and grief in these ways will help you put your life together again. You can't avoid major losses. Important people, places, and stages of life will be lost to you. Having one tragic loss doesn't mean you won't have others, but you can be assured your losses will open new doors as they close old ones.

16

Significant Points along the Way

Mileposts on the road to recovery

Certain points in time after a major loss stand out with special significance. Chapter 5 includes a description of the steps you can expect to take on the way to grief recovery. The following are significant turning points along your way. It helps to think of them as signposts along the road, indicating you have come some distance and are heading in the right direction. Each one represents a time of discovering something new and being challenged to release a part of the past.

The Third Month

The third month after the death of a loved one or the filing of a divorce is often one of the most difficult times of all. By then all vestiges of shock and numbness are gone. The full impact of the loss is upon you.

Enough has happened by this time that denying your loss is impossible. If your spouse died, you have had three full months of filing insurance papers, death certificates, and social-security forms. You have eaten and slept alone for ninety days. If your child died, you know by now that you aren't going to get your little one back. If you have divorced, your ex-spouse may already have a new love interest. The difficult adjustments of this step will persist for some time. But for some reason, the third month will stand out in your mind as the most challenging.

Lori was thirty-five years old when her mother died suddenly. They had lived in different states since Lori and her husband moved away shortly after their marriage. The two women had maintained telephone contact over the years and greatly enjoyed catching up on each other's news each week.

Ninety days after her mother's death, Lori came to see me because she found her thoughts dominated by suicide. She was certain her mother had come to visit her the night before. Her message to Lori was one of loneliness for her and the wish that Lori could be with her.

In the brightness of day, Lori knew her suicidal impulses weren't rational. At night they became more of a problem. I told Lori that what she was experiencing was a normal phenomenon for the third month of her grief recovery. We set up a series of counseling sessions and a procedure for her to call if the night became too difficult.

After meeting several times, I suggested to Lori that she write a letter of good-bye to her mother. (A full discussion of this exercise begins on page 198.) She was to tell her mother how much she loved her, how much she had enjoyed their years together and the special nature of their relationship. But now she had to let her go. Lori had to say good-bye so that she could go on with her life with her husband and family. She would miss her mother very much and would never forget her. She would show gratitude for all her mother had taught her by living a new life with its own fulfillment. After writing the letter, Lori was to read it aloud several times each day until she could get through it without breaking down. Then she was to bring the letter to my office and read it to me.

Lori was able to carry out that difficult task. It proved to be the key in enabling her to put away her self-destructive thoughts. As she faced the reality of her grief and understood more about what to expect of herself, Lori was able to move through it without further threat to herself.

If you are not already in some kind of a support group by the third month, try to find one. It is a time when talking with a professional

The Three-Month Mark

Make a note on your calendar about three months after you experience any significant loss. When some sign of your reaction to it occurs that you didn't expect, you can check the date and say to yourself, "Oh, it's about three months since _____, I'm due for something like this." That simple exercise can turn your normal grief reaction into a time of discovery instead of panic.

counselor or clergyperson is better than the advice of inexperienced friends or family.

Six to Nine Months

This is a special time when you need to focus on the relationship of your body and emotions. Somewhere between six and nine months after a major loss, you could be quite vulnerable to the onset of a serious physical illness. Dr. Glen Davidson's study of bereaved persons indicates about 25 percent of them had a weakened natural immune system during this period. I strongly urge you to mark your calendar at the fifth month and to schedule a doctor's appointment for a physical.

When Pat's husband died, Pat was forced to close a home for runaway youth and move to a new state to find work. She had to say good-bye to friends with whom she had a long and close relationship. Ten months later, Pat developed a mysterious illness. She ran a high fever, suffered from exhaustion, and became too weak to walk without support. Tests revealed an immune deficiency of an unknown classification. In time, the disease disappeared as mysteriously

> I strongly urge you to mark your calendar at the fifth month and to schedule a doctor's appointment for a physical.

as it had appeared. Pat is convinced that grief over her multiple losses lies at the root of this trying experience.

One Year

You don't need to mark the anniversary date of your loss on the calendar. Every widow or widower and every divorced person can tell you the date and hour their loss occurred. You will probably never forget the date of your loss, either.

The one-year anniversary date of a loved one's death is particularly significant. You will have done something you thought was impossible a few months earlier: You will have survived an entire year without someone who was as important to you as life itself.

Many people meet the anniversary date with a mixture of sadness and hope. You are reminded in a vivid way of how much you have lost and how much it still hurts. But you have come through the year, and you are more hopeful for the next one.

After Lucy's husband died, those of us who knew her had a special concern. She didn't seem to be adjusting very well. She came to the grief support group a few times, then dropped out. She appeared to be losing weight and withdrawing from friends and neighbors. She could not dispose of her husband's clothing or a large collection of tools he kept in a metal shed behind their home. She had always taken great pride in her yard. Now it was in shambles.

> Many people meet the anniversary date with a mixture of sadness and hope.

As the anniversary date of her husband's death approached, we were worried. People in the grief support group worked out a plan to have two widows visit her on the morning of the anniversary date. I was to see her in the afternoon. Someone else would invite her to dinner that evening.

When the day arrived, the two women went to see Lucy. They found her out in the yard busily putting in new plants. The tools were gone,

Marking the One-Year Anniversary

You can decide to take charge of this important day. I suggest
- If you work, take the day off. You may want to treat yourself to a night luxuriating at a bed-and-breakfast while someone else cooks your meals.
- Make a conscious effort to recall your loved one.
- Go back in your journal and read your entries for the year. Read your letter of good-bye (see page 198).
- Make phone calls or write notes of thanks to everyone you can think of who was helpful to you throughout the year.
- Arrange a dinner date with a good friend who knows all about your loss.
- Using the exercise for goal setting on page 197, make new plans for the next year.
- If you are living in a new city or state, visit your old home area or call someone you know there.
- Begin studying your new area. Learn something of its history.

sold to a neighbor. The shed was now her garden-supply area. She wasn't home when I went to call because she had gone to a bridge club with a neighbor. At dinner she told her hosts that she had completed her responsibility to mourn and now it was time to get on with her life. She is still a happy and well person who continues to find new ways to enjoy life.

Whatever your loss, make the anniversary a specific time you look forward to with at least as much hope as you give to looking back in sorrow. Mark the date in a special way. You'll find some suggestions for honoring the anniversary in the box above. As you begin the second year after your loss, it is time to focus your attention more on where you are going than where you have been.

The Eighteenth Month

This is the point at which you find out your grief work isn't finished. By the time you are a year and a half away from your loss, you are sure the rough places are behind you. You are having more good days than bad ones. You may have learned to laugh again.

Yet all of a sudden, it may seem as though you are back at the beginning of grief again. Sadness returns. Thoughts of the deceased person dominate your attention. Nights that were finally tolerable get long and tough again. If you are divorced, you may have gone through eighteen months of sheer euphoria at gaining your freedom, only to have the bottom suddenly drop out from under your emotions.

Sadness returns.

As bad as this feels, you are responding in a normal way to a major loss. Very often this is when people turn to a grief support group for the

Intensity of the characteristics of mourning in the first months after the death of a loved one.

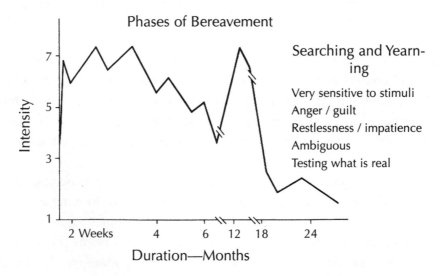

Reprinted by permission from *Understanding Mourning* by Glen W. Davidson ©1984 Augsburg Publishing House.

first time. Dorothy heard about our group from a friend. She walked in one day to say, "I thought I had this thing licked. I never did go through some of the things people told me to expect after my husband's death. Everything was going along fine until early this month. Now I feel like I'm headed backward." When I inquired how long ago Dorothy's husband had died, she told me it had been eighteen months.

Dr. Glen Davidson's study of bereaved people demonstrates the frequency of this return to a more intense level of grieving. The graph above shows that this intensity reappears between the twelfth and eighteenth months after the death of a loved one. The most important things to know about this bump in the road to recovery are

- It is a sign of progress, not regression.
- It doesn't last long.
- The best way to handle it is to do what you would do if the loss were a recent one.

Beyond the Second Year

Once you have passed the second anniversary of your loss, your primary focus will be on adapting to the new life you are finding. Sometimes the greatest challenge is to admit you are ready to move on.

- You may struggle with a sense of being disloyal to a deceased spouse.
- If one of your parents has died and the surviving one begins to date another person or remarries, you may have a problem with anger.
- Parents who lose a child to death often choose this time to begin planning for the birth of another child.

> This is a time to begin making longer-range plans.

- For most divorcing people, the beginning of the third year is when the old marriage is put behind.
- You may begin to waver in your resolve never to marry again.

Beyond the second year you will find that the pain of your grief is not as intense as it had been. Special dates and occasions may still cause you to become emotional, but in general you will be better able to find out what life has in store for you *now*.

This is a time to begin making longer-range plans. It may be the occasion for a new wardrobe or hairstyle. It is a good time to give your loss meaning by using the coping skills you have learned to help others who are grieving.

The End of Grief

It is a terrible lie that says the end of your grief is emptiness and despair. On the contrary, each of the special points in time that we have reviewed here are mileposts along the way to recovery.

You will not always feel as you do in the beginning, middle, or end of grief. If you enter into grief with an understanding of what to expect of yourself, you will find joyful surprises along with the sadness and disappointments.

Grief is not something to avoid. True, it is more difficult and painful than anything else you will face in life. It takes a long time to get through the experience. But grief can also be an unparalleled occasion for discovery of your own strength of character.

The person who drew me into my involvement with grief and loss is Frieda. When her husband died after a lengthy battle with cancer, I expected Frieda to fall apart. George had been one of those big, super-macho men who could do anything. He was a strong personality who dominated his family. Frieda seemed to lean on him for her support, and I wondered how well she would survive George's death.

However, from the beginning, I saw a new Frieda emerge. She became the guiding force in the development of our first grief support group. She helped one newly bereaved person after another see the need to gather together so they could help each other. She encouraged me to risk leading the group. Her open sharing of what she was experiencing week by week taught me my first lesson in understanding the process of healthy grief.

A little more than a year after George's death, Frieda announced to the group that she had remodeled her bedroom. Gone was the massive dark furniture that was characteristic of George. In its place she had a new bed with pink frilly covers, feminine decorations, and new wallpaper.

Frieda's grief was deep and her loss extremely hard for her to handle. But she gave it all she had. In doing so, she found a strength of character that surprised her more than anyone else. Today she is continuing to build a meaningful life for herself.

> Grief is as much about finding as it is about losing.

Frieda found what you can find. Grief is as much about finding as it is about losing. It is not an illness but a process of recovering your balance after life has dealt you a major blow.

Enduring the stresses and challenges of grief recovery calls for a discipline that can add a valuable dimension to your life. You can emerge from it considerably stronger and more compassionate than you were before.

17

Choosing to Live Again

Taking charge of your own grief

As the weeks go by after a major loss, normal routines gradually will re-turn to your life.

If you are employed, the need for income will take you back to work. If you are the parent of young children, you will find their lives go on and so do their demands for attention. Pets still have to be looked after and fed. Bills must be paid. Household tasks and yard work have not taken a vacation while you were in shock.

Granted, nothing is exactly the same as it was before you lost a loved one to death or divorce, or moved to a strange new town, or faced some other major loss. The *tasks* may be the same, but *you* are not!

Work that was all but automatic for you may now seem all but im-possible. The normal cries of your children may grate on your nerves. Routine household chores have become exercises in drudgery.

Your energy level will be very low. You may want excessive amounts of sleep, or lie staring at the ceiling night after night.

As you move beyond the first few weeks, the permanence of your loss comes home, and with that realization comes pain. The usual demands on your life call again for your attention. But now, the pain feels like trying to go through a normal day with the worst toothache you've ever had in your life.

One decision confronts you that dominates all others at this time: You must choose to live again.

Choosing to live again means taking charge of your grief. For the first week or two, much of your life was out of control. Chances are your grief owned you. Now it is time for you to own your grief and to direct the pathway of your recovery.

> Choosing to live again means taking charge of your grief.

You have been knocked off-balance— flattened like a pancake is probably a better description. And now it's time to get up again, recover your sense of balance, and get on with your life.

Giving Yourself Permission to Grieve

This exercise takes grief out of the category of "things that shouldn't happen" and makes it a symbol of your capacity to love.

If you have suffered a major loss recently, grief doesn't seem like something that requires permission. Grief for you is a dirty word; it describes something horrible. It's nothing to be proud of, and you wish it would just go away as quickly as possible.

I want you to give yourself permission to experience another kind of grief. With this exercise you are establishing a purpose for your sadness and taking charge of your own recovery. You will need an 8-½-x-11-inch tablet of lined paper and a pen or pencil.

Follow these steps in exactly the sequence listed.

1. Describe the loss that has brought you grief. How long ago did it happen?
2. Write as much as you want to about the importance of your relationship with that person, place, or condition that is lost.
3. Describe the pain and sadness you feel because of the loss. The list of feeling words in Appendix B may help you describe your feelings more clearly.
4. What is the impact of this loss on your total life? What else have you lost because of this loss?

5. Read your responses to numbers 2, 3, and 4 aloud.
6. What do your responses tell you about your affection for the person, place, or condition that was lost?
7. Considering the love you have for whomever or whatever was lost, and the impact of that loss on your total life, would any other response from you except grief be appropriate?
8. Write the following on a clean sheet of paper:

    The sadness I feel is a badge of honor. I wear the brokenness of my life at this moment with pride. These expressions of my grief testify to the importance of and the depth of my love for _____ (person/ place/condition). I am willing to feel the full impact of my grief as a final act of tribute and love. I will make my way through this experience and will not run from it.

    Sign your name to the statement.
9. Make four copies. Keep the original for yourself and post it in a conspicuous place.
10. Send the copies to four other persons, at least two of whom are not family members. You may want to include your clergy.

Facing a Loss from the Past

If you described an event from the past by several years, you will not re-quire the same amount of time to work through it. However, the grief you are experiencing is no less real.

As you read in Chapter 12, June was more than fifty years old when she first realized she had been sexually molested as a young child. For all those years, the trauma of that terrible event had lain in the recesses of her emotions, too painful to be allowed into consciousness. When the awareness finally came, a deep sadness and grief accompanied it.

Over the course of several months she dug into her painful feelings about her loss. There was no way to recover those lost years or the joy they might have held.

Using a method like the exercise you have just completed, June was able to work through the grief and take charge of her response to a deep wound in her life. Today she has fully recovered her balance in relation to that event. She openly shares her experience to help other women deal with this painful loss. I am very proud of her.

Giving yourself permission to grieve is a great gift. It is an important step in recovering from a present or past loss and an important key to a full life after loss.

Keeping a Journal of Your Journey through Grief

Once you have given yourself permission to grieve, the next important thing for you to do is keep a daily journal of your journey through grief. Use a stenographer's notebook or a diary. Indicate the date and time of the entry at the top of each page. Include this information for each day:

- A significant event that happened
- The person who was most important to me today
- Changes I observe happening to me
- My plans for tomorrow
- Notes to myself

It's a good idea to write in your journal at about the same time every day. This establishes a habit and doesn't require you to think about whether you have made an entry. If you write in your journal at night, do so at least an hour before you plan to go to bed.

The importance of a daily journal will only become evident to you some months, maybe even a year, down the road. The changes that mark your progress through grief come slowly. You may think you are making no progress at all and become more discouraged. At times like these, reading back through your journal will help you remember where you have been and how far you have really come.

The journal helps you stay in charge of your grief experience. It provides guidance for your sharing in your support group and helps you internalize the insights you gain there. There is also some indi-

How Journals Help

- Writing down the events of each day gives these events significance.
- Thinking about people who are important to you keeps you from further loneliness.
- Always noting your plans for the next day encourages a positive direction.

cation that the regular use of a journal may help strengthen your immune system.

I suggest you make your journal entries in the evening because when you are struggling with grief, evenings are almost always the most difficult time of the day. By intentionally focusing on your grief at this time, you take charge of your experience. I call it *de-spooking the evenings*. It works!

It is a good idea to drink only herb teas, decaffeinated coffee, or plain water while you work with your journal. You are doing this in the evening, and caffeinated or high-sugar beverages may interfere with restful sleep later. When you've finished writing in your journal, you may want to read or do some other activity that is relaxing before sleep.

If you have problems relaxing, the next exercises can be helpful. I like them because they are simple and effective.

An Exercise to Relieve Tension

This exercise is known as the *8–8–8 Breather*.

Sit in a comfortable chair with your feet on the floor and your hands laid loosely on your thighs, palms down. Close your eyes. Do the following:

1. Gently blow out all the air in your lungs.
2. Slowly inhale while counting to eight. Allow your abdomen to

expand while you are breathing in. Count: *one-and-two-and-three-and* . . . up to eight.

3. Hold your breath to the same count of eight.
4. Slowly exhale while counting to eight in the same manner. Relax your abdomen as you breathe out.
5. Breathe normally for about one minute.
6. Repeat this sequence several times until you feel your tension subsiding.

A Variation on Counting Sheep

This relaxation exercise can be done any time but is particularly helpful when you can't get to sleep.

Lie down in bed on your back with legs straight and hands by your sides.

Do the 8–8–8 Breather exercise several times.

Close your eyes and look as far up inside your eyelids as you can.

Begin counting silently simultaneously from 1 to 100, and from 100 to 1. It is done like this: 100–1, 99–2, 98–3, 97–4, 96–5. . . . Keep looking up inside your eyelids.

As you continue to count, you will find your eyes becoming tired. Allow them to relax to a comfortable position.

At some point you will begin to have difficulty keeping track of the sequence of numbers. This is a sign your mind is beginning to relax and prepare for sleep. Don't force the sequence to continue.

When this happens, picture yourself at the top of a descending stairway. It is twenty steps in length and is of any design you wish. There is a landing halfway down.

Picture yourself slowly descending the stairs one step at a time. Count them as you go. One-two-three-four . . . . When you reach ten, pause on the landing. Then descend slowly the rest of the way.

You may not reach the bottom before falling asleep. *Don't fight it!*

If you do get all the way to the bottom, you will feel relaxed and at ease. Picture a room that is your own private retreat. No one else ever shares this space with you. It is decorated and arranged exactly as you want it to be. It is warm and comfortable. In this place you are free from all pressures and concerns. Allow yourself to be in this room for as long as you want.

Even if you do not fall asleep, you will be resting. I have found twenty minutes of this kind of relaxation to be as refreshing as two or three hours of normal sleep.

As a variation during the day, you can sit in a comfortable chair, fix your eyes on some small object or mark on a wall, and begin counting until your eyes grow heavy. Then allow your eyes to close, and begin descending the staircase. When you reach your room at the bottom, remain there as long as you wish. When you are ready to end the relaxation period, count your way back up the stairs. Your eyes will open near the top and you will feel quite refreshed and alert.

When You Just Can't Sleep

Sometimes, in spite of your best efforts, you will wake up in the middle of the night and not be able to go back to sleep. It seems to take only a night or two of interrupted sleep to get the cycle started, but it can take months to get back to normal. This exercise will help you reprogram your sleeping habits within a week or two.

First create a daily calendar of the things you are going to do. Divide each twenty-four-hour period into four parts: mornings (after your usual waking time), afternoons, evenings (up to your normal bedtime), and nighttime (normal sleeping hours). Plan your time as follows:

Morning: List what you will do from the time you get up until you have lunch. Schedule your lunch at a specific hour and have it whether you feel like eating or not.

Afternoon: List what you will do after lunch until time for dinner. Also schedule that meal at a specific hour and eat it.

Evening: List the hours of the evening from dinnertime until bedtime. For example, if you eat at 6:00 P.M. and normally go to bed at 10:00 P.M. your schedule would be:

6:00 P.M. Dinner
7:00 P.M.
8:00 P.M.
9:00 P.M.
10:00 P.M. Bedtime

Now fill in what you will do each hour of the evening. Do your best to follow through with each hour's plan.

Nighttime: List the time that you are waking most frequently during the night. Then list each half hour from that time until your normal waking time. For instance, if you normally get up at 6:00 A.M., but now are waking each night at 2:00 A.M., your list would look like this:

2:00 A.M.
2:30 A.M.
3:00 A.M.
3:30 A.M.
4:00 A.M.
4:30 A.M.
5:00 A.M.
5:30 A.M.
6:00 A.M.

Each evening, write down what you will do in thirty-minute increments from the time you wake up until your normal rising time. *This is crucial.* Give yourself tasks to do that are unpleasant. Clean cupboards or toilets, mop floors, balance your checkbook—anything that you do not like to do! There should be no snacking and no lying in bed staring at the ceiling.

If you go back to bed, use one of the relaxation techniques to fall asleep again. Most people find that after a few nights of this regimen they are sleeping until their normal rising time without further problems.

Learning to relax is an important skill to master as you work your way through grief and learn to live again. So is changing your attitude about crying.

A Programmed Cry

This exercise is specifically designed to help you get rid of your fears, fantasies, and reservations about crying. You will probably use it more than once in the first weeks and months after a major loss. It demonstrates clearly that your emotions do not have to be kept under a tight rein, even in the face of the worst of losses.

Preparation

You will be okay when you cry. However, to alleviate any unnecessary anxiety, choose someone to be your caretaker. This person should know what you are doing and be familiar with the circumstances of your grief. Put your caretaker's telephone number by your phone in case you need assistance.

Choose a room in your home that has sentimental importance for you. Supplies should include some large pillows, a full box of tissues, a radio, and photographs of the one who is gone. Do the exercise in the evening.

How to Cry

Turn the lights low. Turn on soft music. Select a station that plays sentimental music with few interruptions, or use records or tapes. Set the volume to a comfortable level, as loud as you like.

Feel the impact of the mood you have created. Allow it to touch your sadness. Think about the person who has died or the dreams for a happy marriage that are gone. Or look at photographs of the people and places you left when you moved to a new city.

Remember the most intimate times. Think about your loss. Turn your feelings loose. Say what you are feeling aloud.

Put two chairs back to back. Sit in one and imagine the person or people you have lost in the other. Talk directly to the one you have lost. Say what you are feeling aloud.

As an alternative, you may want to picture God sitting in the chair. Tell God your feelings about your loss without restraint.

Hold a pillow in your arms and cry into it. Rock back and forth. Yell if you want to. Call out your loss. Feel it completely. Let your feelings go for as long as they want to come out.

Know that you are being healed by the release of all the pain and sadness. Don't try to hide your anger.

When you begin to feel better, allow that new feeling to emerge. Concentrate your attention on the positive thoughts you are having. Say those positive thoughts aloud.

When you are ready, turn up the lights. Turn the music low. Change its mood to something happy and bright. Put away the symbols of your weeping—the tissues, pillow, chairs.

Do breathing exercises, stretch your muscles, do some simple calisthenics, or run in place.

Drink a large glass or two of water. Make some herbal tea or have fruit or vegetable juice. Snack on fresh fruits or vegetables, crackers, pretzels, or popcorn.

Take a warm bath or shower. Read a humorous book. Go to sleep.

As soon as possible, tell your caretaker about the experience. Tell your counselor or grief support group.

Record your experience in your journal.

You will find that most of your hesitancy and discomfort with tears are gone. From now on, you will be able to experience your feelings more easily and with less anxiety.

Many people have found this exercise to be like turning on the lights in a dark room. All the mystery and myth associated with the act of crying disappears. Instead of tears being a problem for you in working through your grief, they become a resource for healing. Once you are more comfortable with crying, you are ready to confront your grief in a more direct way.

Communicating with Your Grief

This exercise does for grief what the last one did for crying. It dispels the notion that grief is a six-headed monster that will "get you" if you mention its name. The task here is to communicate with your grief as though it has its own personality. You will talk to your grief and you will listen to your grief.

If your loved one has died, this is an especially helpful exercise about three months after the death.

You will write two letters. I suggest using whatever stationery you normally use for writing to friends or family. See pages 97 and 98 for examples.

The first letter is from you to your grief. Use the following form:

Date: Time:
To Grief,

Sincerely,
(your name)

Before you write, ask yourself, "If I could tell my grief what I am thinking and feeling, what would I say? What do I want my grief to know about its effect on my life?"

Be as frank as you can. Write the letter and sign it.

As close as possible to twenty-four hours later, but no less than that, write the second letter. This one will be from your grief to you.

Use the same format as the first letter, except address it to yourself and sign it "Sincerely, Grief."

Before writing, ask yourself: What do I think my grief is telling me? What does it want from me?

Then, as frankly as possible, write to yourself on behalf of your grief.

Put the letters aside for a day or two, then read them both aloud to yourself.

What do the letters reveal about your attitude toward the experience of grief? What new thing can you learn about yourself from the letters?

Find someone with whom you can share the letters and talk about your discoveries. If you are in a support group, this is an excellent activity to share with each other.

I suggest you keep your letters with your journal.

About two years later, write the same letters again without referring to the originals, then compare your responses. You will be amazed that the same person wrote both sets of letters! You may find the second set sound as though they were written by an adventurer rather than a person who is grieving.

> About two years later, write the same letters again without referring to the originals, then compare your responses.

If communicating with your grief is a problem, communicating with your friends, family, and co-workers will be, too. There aren't many people around who will be comfortable with your grief. Very soon after any major loss, including death and divorce, folks will want you at least to act as if you are choosing to live again. They will want you to do this long before you are ready for it.

Anthropologist Margaret Mead said, "When a person is born we celebrate; when they marry we are jubilant; but when they die, we act as if nothing has happened." Why? Because birth and marriage are occasions when loss is dominated by joyful gain. We know what to say and how to react in those occasions. But we see death as canceling every aspect of human joy. We don't know what to say to a bereaved person. We are terribly uncomfortable in the presence of someone else's grief.

That's good to remember when it's our turn to grieve. When people stay away at the time we need them most, it's not that they don't love us. They just don't know what to say or do. They feel helpless.

The next exercise is designed to help you communicate with those whose support you need the most. This includes family members, friends, clergy, and doctors.

What to Remember about People Who Aren't Grieving

Type or write the following sentences on a card or piece of paper and carry it with you for the first nine months of your grief experience.

1. I will not expect others to be better at handling my grief than I would have been at handling theirs before my loss.
2. People cannot be something other than who they are.
3. Most people want to help me. They mean well even when they do dumb and hurtful things.
4. Others, including professional people, will not know what is helpful to me unless I tell them.
5. I will be as patient with others as I need them to be with me.

Carry this information with you so it is readily available. You will want to read it for comfort several times each day because other people will do incredibly uncaring things quite innocently. For example, if your spouse has died, it won't be long before somebody:

- Asks how you are doing, and you will sense the only acceptable answer is "fine."
- Acts as if your deceased husband or wife never had a name. This will happen at a time when you want everyone to know that he or she was a special person who will always be a part of your life.
- Finds a way to avoid talking to you.
- Questions some decision you made about the funeral, burial, or events preceding the person's death.

If you understand that other people's poor reactions are not your fault, you will be spared one more burden from the load you are already carrying.

Things to Tell Nongrievers

Have the following statements typed or printed on good-quality colored paper. A quick-print store can do it for you. Almost every town has one, and it has all the supplies you need.

> My dear _____ (Family, Friends, Pastor, Employer . . .),
>
> I have experienced a loss that is devastating to me. It will take time, perhaps years, for me to work through the grief I feel because of this loss.
>
> I will cry more than usual for some time. My tears are not a sign of weakness or a lack of hope or faith. They are the symbols of the depth of my loss and the sign that I am recovering.
>
> I may become angry without seeming to have a reason for it. My emotions are heightened by the stress of grief. Please be forgiving if I seem irrational at times.
>
> I need your understanding and your presence more than anything else. If you don't know what to say, just touch me or give me a hug to let me know you care. Please don't wait for me to call you. I am often too tired to even think of reaching out for the help I need.
>
> Don't allow me to withdraw from you. I need you more than ever during the next year.
>
> Pray for me only if your prayer is not an order for me to make you feel better. My faith does not excuse me from the grief process.
>
> If you have had an experience of loss that seems anything like mine, please share it with me. You will not make me feel worse.
>
> This loss is the worst thing that could happen to me. But I will get through it and I will live again. I will not always feel as I do now. I will laugh again.
>
> Thank you for caring about me. Your concern is a gift I treasure.
>
> *Sincerely,*
> *(your name)*

Alter this sample letter in whatever way suits your circumstances. Give a copy to those whose support you need most. By putting thoughts such as these in writing you will avoid much misunderstanding. People will know better what to expect from you.

With this letter, you also affirm in a strong way that you intend to be in charge of your grief experience and to grow through it.

Getting on with Life

Making the decision to live again after a major loss is not easy. It requires putting your willpower and thought-power ahead of some very intense emotions.

You cannot wait until you feel better and then decide to live again. You must make the decision intellectually because you know it's right, and then wait for your feelings to catch up. They will.

The next chapter contains more exercises to help you carry out your decision and establish a high-quality new life after your loss.

Taking a Time-Out

It's okay and wise to take an occasional time-out from the heavy business of grieving. To do so doesn't dishonor one who has died or indicate any lack of concern for the loss that has taken place. It does provide an opportunity, if only for a few hours or minutes, to go through the motions of a normal life again.

The following exercise comes from a friend who is both a skilled bereavement counselor and a survivor of multiple major losses. It works wonders!

> It's okay and wise to take an occasional time-out from the heavy business of grieving.

Fun Things To Do

Do one or more of the following on a given day.

1. Go to an ice cream store and taste every flavor they have. (Tasting is free.)
2. Take a giant stuffed animal to a supermarket. Put it in your cart and push it around as you shop. You will be amazed and uplifted by the response of other shoppers.
3. Go to the classiest hotel you can find. Walk around as if you were staying there, being sure to window shop the gift store.
4. Go to art galleries, antique stores, flea markets, or book stores. Just "hang out" and browse.
5. Go to a mall. Measure the time it takes for you to walk it completely. When finished, treat yourself to a goodie.
6. Go fly a kite.
7. Find a park with a duck pond and feed the ducks.
8. Plant a small garden. An herb garden in a pot works fine.
9. Create your own potpourri. Simmer and enjoy its fragrance.
10. Read poetry out loud. It's best done with another person— even over the telephone.
11. Put up a hummingbird feeder.
12. Take yourself on a picnic. If weather doesn't permit being outdoors, do it on the floor of your house, complete with picnic ware.
13. Put on a musical CD or tape that you enjoy. Turn it up loud and sing along. (It's good if you can sing, better if you can't.)
14. Take a child to the zoo or a carnival. Eat cotton candy together.
15. Start a humor scrapbook. Read the cartoon section of your paper and cut out the best.

18

Opening New Doors

Decisions that make a difference

Decision making is one of the most difficult challenges you will face as you work at recovering your balance after a major loss. In the first few days you operate like a robot as you face endless demands. You go through the motions of decision making.

Later, the numbness and shock wear off and you experience excruciating pain. Making *any* decision takes maximum effort. At first, the decisions are impossible to avoid: There is the paperwork that follows a death or divorce or the tasks of locating necessary services in a new town, or adjusting to life without one of your limbs, for example.

Still later, decision making has a new dimension. The pressure now is not so much what you *have to do* as what you *want to do*. You recognize it is time to move on. Your challenge is one of motivation. You may not feel like getting out of bed, getting dressed, eating, or leaving the house. This is a time when many people find volunteering provides the reason they need to go on with a normal life.

Carl found himself deeply depressed after his wife's death. He could not make himself go about any of his usual activities. Then a friend suggested he volunteer at a local blood bank. Having a responsibility to be someplace at a certain time and feeling a sense of satisfaction in helping others gave Carl the motivation he needed to get back into life.

Like Carl, you may find that the pain continues even with volunteer work. You are fairly sure the emptiness and sadness in the pit of your stomach and the ache in your heart will be part of your life for a long time. But at least now you have a reason for living. As you give yourself to some task that benefits others, life is simply more bearable.

Six months after her husband died, Cindy came to see me in a new state of shock. A man in her office had asked her for a date! The fact that she now had a decision to make stunned her. She was single, but she didn't think of herself that way. Like most widows, she differed from divorced singles in that she saw herself as a married person whose husband was dead. Her divorced friends saw themselves as single and available to the right person.

For Cindy, the difficulty in saying "yes" or "no" to a date was that either answer acknowledged she now had decisions to make and a life to live without Hal. I think that's also the reason so many divorced persons are crushed by the news of their ex-spouse's remarriage. It drives home the fact that the past is really *gone*. It cannot be recovered, and life must now go on.

There comes a time in recovering from the grief of any major loss when you will seem to be standing in a large, cold room with no windows and many, many doors. You will know that you must leave this room sometime. It is not a pleasant place, but nevertheless, choosing a door isn't easy.

The room is filled with the memories and images of your past and the terrible loss you have experienced. You aren't sure that what waits beyond any of the doors is better. You hope so, but you can't see how life can ever be warm and cozy again.

To leave the room is to leave your past. You can take your memories with you, but that's all.

Any choice you make will take you on to a new and different life that you have never lived before.

It's time to choose.

Earl Grollman says in his book *Time Remembered:*

It's a risk to attempt new beginnings . . . . Yet the greater risk is for you to risk nothing. For there will be no further possibilities of learning and changing, of traveling upon the journey of life . . . . You were strong to hold on. You will be stronger to go forward to new beginnings.[1]

An Exercise in Setting Goals

In your journal or on a separate tablet, put the date at the top of a page and answer these questions.

1. What tasks do I need to complete in the next seven days? If I didn't have to do these things, what would I *like* to do in the next seven days?
2. What barriers keep me from doing what I most want to do?
3. What resources do I have to overcome these barriers?
4. Whose help do I need to do the things I want to do?
5. What things would I like to do in the next ninety days?
6. What spiritual resources do I need to find or recover to help me go on with my life?
7. What would my life look like one year from today if I could have my way?

Choose one goal each from your seven-day, ninety-day, and one-year lists. Write down each of these goals and indicate how you will know when you have reached each of them:

Seven days
Ninety days
One year

Select one spiritual resource you would like to find or recover. Make an appointment to discuss this goal with your minister, priest, or rabbi. If you do not belong to a religious community, ask a friend for a referral.

Make a diary notation on your calendar to check on your seven-day goal one week from this date.

Begin working on each of the goals you selected no later than one day after the date on the top of your questionnaire.

Keep a record in your journal of your progress on each of the goals you selected. If you accomplish one, choose another from the same category. If it becomes obvious that a goal is unrealistic, choose an alternate. If a new goal surfaces, go for it!

Share your goals and the dates for completion with a friend who will hold you accountable.

At the end of the first week, set a new goal for the next seven days. Continue this procedure for at least the first year.

> By setting short-, medium-, and long-range goals for yourself, you begin to open the doors to your future.

By setting short-, medium-, and long-range goals for yourself, you begin to open the doors to your future. Whether you reach all of the goals doesn't matter. The important thing is that you are beginning to make new choices for your life after loss.

The next step is a painful one. I want you to know that up-front, before you begin the exercise. It is also a very important step to your continued recovery.

Writing a Letter of Good-bye

Saying good-bye is never easy. Whether guests go home or you leave favorite relatives after a visit, the time of parting has an element of sadness to it.

To say good-bye to a deceased loved one, the end of a marriage, or the places and people you called home hurts beyond words.

However, before you can open new doors for your life, you have to close the doors that now lead to the past. It doesn't mean forgetting the person or memories any more than you forget your friends when they go home after dinner at your house.

To say good-bye acknowledges you will not share life with a person, place, stage of life, or part of your body anymore.

Writing this letter is an act of lovingly releasing a part of your life that will always remain important to you in memory, but which you must now live without.

It is important to say good-bye as you part temporarily from folks you care about. It's even more important to say good-bye to those whom you will not see again in this life. It is just as important to bid good-bye to lost places and dreams.

Because you can't say good-bye in person to the one who has died or the marriage that has ended, the next alternative is to write a letter. If you are like most people who have done this, it will be the most difficult letter you have ever written. It helps to remember this is also one of the most important letters you will ever write.

To begin, think about whomever or whatever was lost to you that is the source of your grief. Go back to your journal and look at

> This letter deserves the best you've got.

what you wrote in the exercise called "Giving Yourself Permission to Grieve" (page 180).

Use your favorite stationery for this letter. If you don't have a supply, buy some as though you were writing to someone very important. Use a good pen. This letter deserves the best you've got. No pencils or notebook paper, please.

Address your letter as follows: If it is to a deceased person, use the salutation you used in life with this person. If it is to a marriage that is now over, address the focus of your loss, as if it were a person. That may or may not be your ex-spouse. It may be your mutual friends, the traditions surrounding the holidays, or the effect on your children. If it is to a place, address the letter as if it were to a person. (June and I wrote to "Our Dear Home. . . . ") If it is an unfulfilled goal, a business failure, or a stage of your life, address it in a personal way.

After addressing your letter, immediately acknowledge that this is a letter of farewell. Then proceed to tell the person or personalized event anything you would like to have said, but didn't.

> Read the letter aloud several times each day for several days.

- Express thanks for specific things you will remember. If you are writing to a deceased loved one, give your permission for that person to be dead.
- Share your hopes and vision for the life you will live after your loss.

Sign the letter in whatever way is appropriate for you. Wait about one day and then read your letter aloud to yourself. Read it aloud several times each day for several days. When you can read it all the way through, even with tears, read it aloud to a friend, counselor, or clergy.

Keep the letter with your journal and other written exercises as an example of a historic moment along your journey to recovery.

Ken wrote the following as part of his letter after the death of his wife:

> My darling Mae,
> You and I always had our Lord with us. If it weren't so, I don't know what I would do now. That is what sustained us through your illness and now my faith and trust in my beloved Lord is what sustains me.
>
> The great void your death has left in my life is still a gaping hole. How can a "we" become an "I"? How can an "us" become a "me"? How can an "our" become a "mine"?
>
> Because of God, I believe there will always be a "we" and an "us" and an "our" in my heart. By faith I can release you to the love and care of our Lord until we will meet again in his Kingdom.
>
> *Ken*

This letter helped Ken release his attachment to Mae and move on to a new life for himself that in time included another wife.

Martha's loss was the marriage she thought would last forever. After eleven years, it was over. She and Brad had shared a common dream for the first few years. As they struggled through a career change for him, she worked to help support them, sacrificing her own vocational goals.

She imagined that once he was established in his new career, it would be her turn to return to school. When the day came that Brad had a good job with a promising future in front of them, Martha quit her job and enrolled in night school. Brad was furious. He wanted her to work until their debt for his education was paid off. Their fights over money spread to the subject of having children. He was ready. She wasn't.

Outwardly they looked like an ideal couple. In private, the words between them grew ever more harsh, and the happy times became rare. It all ended when Martha came home unexpectedly in the middle of the day to find Brad in bed with another woman.

After the divorce became final, I suggested Martha write a letter of good-bye to Brad and their marriage. At first, I think she was sure I had lost my mind. In time, Martha did write the letter. Here is an excerpt:

> Bradley,
>
> As I write this letter to say good-bye to you, I refuse to add the word, "Dear." I don't think I will ever forgive you for what you did to me, although I'm told this anger I feel will be more costly to me than to you. It's hard for me to remember that the first six years of our marriage were so good. I think it's knowing that once I loved you so much (and I think you loved me too) that hurts the most.
>
> It feels as if something inside of me has been murdered. I feel so sad and so angry, all at the same time. My only hope is that one day I will be able to remember the good times without having my thoughts dominated by the ugliness of the last two years.
>
> I am trying to put my life together again. I have started going to church again and that gives me some peace, at least for a little while. I am going to night school and doing well and that helps me to feel better about myself.
>
> I don't miss you and all the hassles, but I do hate being alone so much. I can't even stand the thought of getting involved with another man. He'd probably turn out to be like you. Maybe someday. First, I will get to know me and what I want much better than I do now.
>
> I believe there is a good life for me in the future because I believe I am a good person.
>
> Brad, this is hard for me to say, but thanks for the early years. Our picnic breakfasts in the park and laughter we shared about our first little apartment are memories I want to keep.
>
> Good-bye. I hope you will remember some good things about being with me, too.
>
> *Martha*

By reading her letter aloud several times, Martha was able to iden-tify her anger and begin the process of releasing it. Over the next sev-eral months she was able to see more of her own failure in the marriage. In time she received a college degree and she is now doing well in her career. When I last saw her, Martha was still single.

Using the Resources of Religion

Regardless of whether you have been an actively religious person in the past, religious resources are important for you now. The resources that religion offers best are hope, comfort, and a sense of some greater meaning to life. You will benefit from all of these as you begin to open new doors to your life.

> The resources that religion offers best are hope, com-fort, and a sense of some greater meaning to life.

Grief is not foremost an intellectual experience. Philosophical religious con-cepts won't help you. This is no time for theological debates about the "right" kind of religion.

I urge you to find the clergyperson and church or synagogue in your area that has the best program for grief support. Whatever the religious orientation of the group, it will help you.

Starting a Grief Support Group

The best support system while working through your grief is a group of people who have also experienced loss. One new door you can choose to open is organizing and starting such a group. It may sound difficult, but I assure you it isn't.

Loss and grief are such common experiences that announcing almost anywhere that you are forming a support group will produce the people you need. A group doesn't have to be larger than three or four and should not exceed eight or ten people without a trained leader.

When someone's grief becomes distorted, the group provides a lov-ing atmosphere in which it is okay to urge that person to seek profes-sional counseling.

The exercises I have described in this book are useful as group activities. All of them have been tested over a minimum of ten years in groups I have led.

Your church or synagogue can be an excellent source of people for the group. Your pastor, priest, or rabbi may provide a meeting place and perhaps help with leadership.

How long should you have a support group? The answer is, as long as you feel the need and until you have opened all the doors to new life that you want to open. A grief support group should

> A grief support group doesn't require a highly trained, professional leader to be effective. It is an added bonus if one is available, especially as the group gets started. You may be able to find a counselor who will act as a referral resource if someone in the group shows signs of distorted grief.

plan to meet for a minimum of twelve sessions on a weekly basis for one to one and a half hours per session. I personally like the ongoing model, in which people can attend for as long as they wish. This model also provides a ready-made referral place for newly bereaved persons.

Remember, the entire first year after a major loss is dominated by experiences of "the first time without." For at least that year you need all the support you can get.

A support group also gives your own loss meaning because you are using your experience to help others. That's no little thing!

Appendix C contains a more detailed description of how to call a group together and what to do during the first few sessions.

Turning Your Loss into a Creative Hurt

When you get involved with the grief of other people, you should know one thing: Sharing in the grief of others is like playing in the mud. You can't do it without getting some on you!

> Loss and grief are such common experiences that announcing almost anywhere that you are forming a support group will produce the people you need.

At times, you will be sure you have all you can carry with your own grief. You won't see how you could handle that of anyone else in addition.

However, there is a marvelous mystery about grief: The more you share in the grief of others, the more in charge of your own grief you will be. It won't be any less painful. But it will seem considerably more manageable.

> The more you share in the grief of others, the more in charge of your own grief you will be.

When you share your struggles and discoveries with others and listen to their stories, you will find your pain becoming a *creative hurt*—an experience you can learn from. It will have purpose, meaning, and a dignity that you didn't sense before.

The people I know who have most fully recovered their balance after a major loss are those who gave the most of themselves to others.

Jeanne lost her husband of forty-nine years after a brief illness. She was past seventy at the time. They had no children. Shortly after Alan's death, Jeanne began pouring her life into the needs of others. She befriended a young mother whose husband committed suicide, cared for a sister until her death at age ninety-three, and became the source of hope for another widow who was struggling with a drinking problem. She was past age eighty-five when she volunteered at a community food bank and served on the council for a preschool.

Mary, widowed many years younger than Jeanne, has become a volunteer in the surgery waiting room of the hospital where her husband died. Dorothy, whose husband has been a victim of Alzheimer's disease for several years, fills the loneliness of her life by volunteering at a local school. She works as a teacher's aide with first graders who dearly love her attention.

> A creative hurt is a painful experience you can learn from.

Al poured himself into volunteer work at his church after his wife's death to cancer. He sings in the choir, helps in the office, and chairs the personnel committee.

The opportunities and the needs are endless. It's another step on the path to recovery that's often difficult to take, but the rewards are plentiful. I can't diagram an exercise to tell you how to turn the pain of your grief into a creative hurt. I can only tell you that the opportunities are there if you will open the doors before you.

Another door that is always before you some time after a major loss is the need to give forgiveness to someone. A failure to open this door can block your ability to release the past and move fully into a new life.

An Exercise in Forgiveness

Two almost surefire spin-offs of grief are anger and broken relationships. It is as true in the case of a death as it is with a divorce. It is a factor in relocation and other major losses.

I believe you can make the following assumption and never be wrong: *If you have experienced grief, there is someone you need to forgive.*

> If you have experienced grief, there is someone you need to forgive.

It's possible, of course, that there is someone who needs to forgive you. But that is *their* task. Your need to forgive is *your* task. Granting forgiveness is another way to open a door in your life and move forward.

Begin with this survey, using a clean piece of paper. At the top, write the name of a person with whom you have had conflict or from whom you have felt alienated since your loss. Write down your answers to the following questions:

- What is your relationship with this person? Is he or she a family member or friend? How long have you known this person?
- Do you blame this person in any way for your loss? If so, how?
- Are you angry, resentful, or hateful toward this person? If so, why?
- What is happening to you because of the break in your relationship with this person?

- Can you forgive this person and express your forgiveness? If you are able to forgive, write down a date on which you will offer your forgiveness. Also note if you will express it in person, on the telephone, or by letter.

Granting forgiveness is never easy and can be especially difficult when grief is involved. You may think you would be disloyal to the one who has died or disloyal to your own principles if there has been a divorce. You may feel vulnerable or fear looking weak.

If your anger is still unresolved and you are unable to consider forgiveness, continue this exercise, using another piece of paper. Answer these questions:

- How is your self-esteem being affected by your anger? In what ways are you being robbed of energy? Is your sleep being affected?
- Write down the name of a trusted friend, counselor, or clergy. Share this survey and your struggle to forgive with this person.
- Determine why you are not able to forgive. Find the deeper reasons for your hurt and anger.
- Write a letter of forgiveness to the person whether or not you feel forgiving. Write as if you want to forgive. Place the letter in an envelope and put it in your journal. As you make your journal entry each day, read the letter aloud to yourself. Make changes in the letter as your feelings change. Stay with it until you can begin to feel forgiving.

Do not mail the letter or act on it until you are sure you are fully ready to forgive. I suggest choosing an occasion that has special meaning on which to act on your forgiveness.

Reaching out with forgiveness will bring more healing to you than to the one you forgive.

The Importance of Touch

During those first few days after your loss, when shock and numbness have shut down your emotional system, nothing will communicate caring to you quite as much as the touch of another person. Over the course of the ensuing months, you will appreciate those people who don't try to find the right words to say but are present with a touch on the arm or a timely hug.

The touch of another human being counts more when you have experienced a major loss than at any other time in your life.

I learned this while on call to a local hospital. My staff and I were providing supplemental pastoral services to the one full-time Protestant chaplain. The first emergency call I received was to the infant intensive-care unit.

A baby had been born prematurely and wasn't making it on his own. When I arrived, the newborn was hooked to special machines that helped him breathe and monitored his every function. After some time it was clear that he simply was not developed enough to survive.

The time had come to make the decision to unhook the life support. I held hands with the parents as the wires and tubes were removed. We took the baby to the mother's room, where each of us took turns holding him, stroking him, and crying while he died.

I had never had that experience before. At first it seemed cruel to me to subject the parents to holding their dying baby. It took only the first few seconds of my turn to hold the child to realize the wisdom of the experience.

He was not a fetus or an "it." He was a real person, worthy of love and worthy of grief because he was dying. It felt good to hold him and cry and tell his parents how beautiful he was. The mother and father unwrapped him from his blanket, admired each finger and toe, and gave him the only caresses they would ever be able to give.

I talked to those parents several times over the next months. They mourned their son in an appropriate way, but they were also proud of him. He was theirs. They had touched him. He had touched *them.*

I had touched him, too, and been touched by him. In some way I will never understand fully, I am a better minister and a more compassionate person because of that baby who lived in this world only a few hours. I know it happened because we touched.

I'm telling you this in the hope you will be motivated to touch and be touched, even at those points in your grief recovery when you are most inclined to withdraw. One of those times is often about the third month after your loss. Another is between the ninth and twelfth months. Another is at or near the eighteenth month.

You may think that touching or hugging is no more appropriate at these times than I did in that hospital. I want you to know it is not only appropriate, it is great for you!

I now close every session of our grief support group by gathering the people in a close circle where we hold hands as we have a prayer. I think the touch is as vital to our well-being as the prayer.

I also find myself hugging widows, widowers, parents who have lost children, those who come for counseling because of divorce, and everyone who has suffered a loss and comes to talk to me about it. I haven't met most of them before the occasion. I have never been refused or put off.

Dr. Leo Buscaglia has taught that hugs are good medicine for whatever ails us. They can be lifesavers when we are struggling with grief.

Making Peace with Grief

This exercise requires the help of a friend with a pleasant, soothing voice. Its purpose is to help you become more at peace with your grief and feel more free to open the doors to a new life. You will need a cassette-tape recorder and a blank tape.

Ask your friend to record the following message, reading it exactly as it is written. The narrator should speak in a soothing voice at a moderate rate of speed. Wherever three dots appear (. . .), it means to be silent for about three seconds before going on. The easiest way to time the silence is to count slowly and silently *one-and-two-and-three*.

Before you listen to the tape, please take a moment to get relaxed. Sit upright in a comfortable chair with your feet on the floor and your hands held loosely in your lap. Take off your shoes, remove your glasses, and loosen any tight clothing. Be sure you will not be interrupted by the telephone or other distractions.

The narrator will record this message, which you will play back on the recorder:

> . . . Please focus your attention on your breathing. Notice how breathing slowly and rhythmically helps you relax . . . Take a few deep breaths . . . Very good . . .

Before you listen to the tape, please take a moment to get relaxed.

Now take what we will call *a peaceful breath*. It's a special kind of deep breath that will tell your body and mind it's time to be at peace. The peaceful breath is taken like this:

Breathe out all of the air from your lungs. Inhale slowly through your nose to a count of eight . . . Blow the breath out forcefully through your mouth.

You will note a sensation of tingling after two or three peaceful breaths . . . That is your sign that you are relaxing deep inside.

Continue to breathe slowly and deeply, breathing in through your nose and out through your mouth. As you do this, close your eyes, if you have not already done so . . . Good . . . Now, with your eyes closed, turn your eyes as far to the left as you can, as though you were going to look out your left ear. Keep looking to the left as hard as you can . . . You may notice that your eye muscles and eyelids have become quite tense . . .

That's good, because I want you to experience the difference between tension and peacefulness. When I count to three, allow your eyes to come back to the front and feel the tension disappear. One . . . Two . . . Three . . .

Feel the soothing peacefulness around your eyes and in the back of your neck . . . Continue to breathe slowly and deeply . . . In through your nose, out through your mouth . . .

Begin to relax all the muscles in your face . . . around your eyes . . . in your cheeks . . . your forehead . . . your scalp . . . down to your mouth and chin . . . You may find your mouth dropping open a bit . . . That's fine . . . Keep breathing in the same manner . . . in through your nose, out through your mouth . . .

Allow your neck muscles to relax . . . Your head is tipping forward . . . You are feeling the relaxation and peacefulness moving to your shoulders . . . across your back . . . down to the middle of your back . . . down to your lower back . . .

Allow this same peacefulness to flow through your arms to your hands and fingers . . . down each leg and into your feet and toes. Continue to breathe slowly and deeply in through your nose, out through your mouth.

You may become aware of your heartbeat . . . Some people say they feel or hear the blood moving in their arteries. Whatever you are feeling is your body's way of being relaxed and at peace . . .

Start back at the top of your head and do a peacefulness checklist . . . Can you find any place where you are still holding tension? . . . If so, allow that tension to leave . . .

As you continue to be relaxed and at peace . . . The most peaceful you have felt in a long time . . . Concentrate again on your breathing . . . Say to yourself with each exhale, *more relaxed* . . .

When you are fully relaxed . . . Take time to enjoy the feeling . . . Allow your body to enjoy the sense of peacefulness . . . Let it into your stomach and intestines . . .

As you are in this very peaceful, relaxed state, allow your grief to join you . . . It is not the hurtful, painful thing it was . . . but a natural part of life . . . You are at peace with your grief as you are with your natural body. Continue your breathing . . .

Allow your imagination to create a new life for you as you would like it to be in the future . . . See all the possibilities for you. Focus on your wish for yourself . . . As you breathe, tell yourself with every breath, *I will fulfill my dream* . . . Add anything else you want to say to yourself . . .

As you end this exercise, you will find that you are as refreshed as if you have had a restful sleep . . . You will be relaxed and yet full of energy . . . You will have a new sense of well-being and a new resolve for your life . . .

You can come back to this very peaceful state any time you want to by using your peaceful breathing . . . Now, breathing in an easy, normal way, as I count backward from five to one, you will open your eyes and be fully alert . . . Five . . . Four . . . Three . . . Two . . . One. . . . Very good!

You can play this tape for yourself as often as you like. It is the most effective anytime after the ninth month after your loss.

By the time you reach the point of opening new doors for your life, you not only deserve a sense of peacefulness, but also the right to spoil yourself just a bit.

The suggestions in the box on this page are made to help you take care of yourself. Your imagination may inspire you to add others to the list.

It's Okay to Live Again

Some actions you can take are relatively simple but carry strong symbolic images of opening new doors:

- Change your hairstyle to something quite different.
- Make it one hundred percent your choice!
- Have yourself color-draped. This means having a skilled person help you choose the best wardrobe colors to complement your skin tone and hair. Buy some new clothes in your best color.
- Go on a trip you have wanted to take but couldn't because of responsibilities you no longer have.
- Remodel one room in your house to suit you. Sometimes just paint or wallpaper and a few accessories can do wonders.
- Change your mealtime routine, including the time. Many widowed persons find that sitting in their spouse's place at the table eases the loneliness.

19

Your Own Best Friend

Completing the journey

Nobody likes to lose. Losing always hurts, whether it is a little loss and a little hurt or a loss equal to the death of your child and a great big hurt.

If you are a normal, healthy person, you want to be a winner. You grew up liking success stories. You were taught to believe bigger is best, more is better, and getting is much more fun than losing.

Somewhere along the way you had a minor loss. It was one of those disappointments that can "ruin" your life for at least forty-eight hours. A well-meaning friend asked, "What did you do to deserve that?" You were pretty sure you must have done something.

Now you have had a major loss. It has affected your life for more than a year. Grief has become your constant companion. It has drained your emotions and robbed you of joy.

You have experienced grief for only one reason. You are alive. You don't deserve the pain or exhaustion, the emptiness, sadness, or frustration that accompanies grief. I hope you know by now that God did not will your loss. There is not some divine justice system that has punished you for your mistakes.

As long as you are alive, you will experience loss from time to time. Some losses will be small and you will soon forget them. Others will change the course of your life.

> As long as you are alive, you will experience loss from time to time.

When you pass the anniversary date of a major loss in your life, there is at least one good thing to say: *You made it!* This seems especially true when your grief is due to death or divorce.

It is finally up to you whether your major losses destroy you or help you grow into a stronger, better person. No one can make you grow through loss, but nothing can keep you from growth either. When you say, "I made it through this year," you will be acknowledging the greatest accomplishment of your life.

> Somewhere between the first and second anniversaries of your loss you will discover a new best friend—yourself.

You have been in the depths. You have faced the worst experiences in your life. You have endured more emotional pain longer than you dreamed you could. You have made decisions that a few months earlier were unthinkable. In the midst of your own hurt, you have reached out to others who were also grieving.

Now you are beginning to look at the possibilities of a new life. You didn't ask for a new life. You didn't want it. But now that it's here, you will make the most of it. It seems to offer its own joys.

In spite of the ongoing loneliness, you are regaining your balance in life. Having gone through the most difficult places along the way of grief recovery, you know yourself better than you ever did before. As you build your new life after loss, you need to be especially aware of your current strengths and weaknesses.

The exercise "Best Friend–Worst Enemy" should help you identify both more clearly. Refer to the box on the opposite page for this exercise.

As you continue to work through your loss and grief, the tasks before you in the second year will not be as crushing as those that are behind you. Your most difficult period will probably be somewhere around the eighteenth month, when some of the old restlessness and impatience may return. As I said before, it won't last. You now also have your newly found best-friend self to help you past this bump in your road to recovery.

Best Friend–Worst Enemy

Divide a sheet of 8-½ x-11–inch paper in half vertically by folding it or drawing a line from top to bottom.

On the left side at the top, write "Worst Enemy." On the right side, write "Best Friend."

Now reflect on the following statements:

- *There is some way in which each of us is our own worst enemy; likewise, there is some way in which each of us is our own best friend.*

or

- *As our own worst enemy, we create inner conflicts and make it more difficult to do the things we want or need to do.*
- *As our own best friend, we bring special skills, gifts, and qualities to whatever we are doing.*

On the left side of the paper, list the ways in which you are your own worst enemy.

On the right side, list the ways in which you are your own best friend.

Examine both lists. In what ways can your "best friend" help your "worst enemy"?

Could your worst-enemy traits be helped by a professional counselor? If so, seek that help. Share your lists with your grief support group, clergy, or counselor.

If you are recovering from the death of your spouse or a divorce, most of your energies will be devoted to finding ways to shake off the loneliness. Other major losses can leave you facing the same task. Here is a three-word formula for shaking off loneliness: *Release . . . Reorient . . . Reconnect.*

Release

It is painful to release the emotional ties to that part of your life that has been lost, but you will never fully recover your balance until you do.

- It may seem disloyal or sinful even to think about another person after your spouse has died. You may feel guilty when you first begin to enjoy life again.
- Your load of disillusionment after a broken marriage may be overwhelming.
- It's rough to let go of sentimental attachments to the place where you spent a significant portion of your life.

Nevertheless, this letting go of the past is crucial to moving on to a future life after your loss.

One image that has helped many widowed persons let go of the past is to pretend the circumstances are reversed. That is, pretend you are the one who has died. If that were the case and you were aware of your spouse's grief, what would you wish for him or her? Would you wish for a lifetime of sadness, depression, and loneliness? Not at all! The two of you have spent years caring for one another. You would wish for your spouse to be happy again. Try to imagine your spouse wishing the same for you.

> To release your attachment doesn't mean to forget or to deny the importance of that part of your life.

Think about your loss. Is it now time for you to release your emotional attachment to whomever or whatever was lost? To the marriage that is never going to be fulfilled? To a stage of life in which you found special meaning? To some other loss?

Rhonda and Bill had both been married before. They were good for each other during the brief time of their marriage before he died of cancer. She took care of him at home until the end, using her professional nursing skills to enable him to die with dignity.

Alan and Margaret lived in the same community. They had shared life together for more than forty years before she died of cancer. Her deterioration was extremely difficult for Alan to accept. He called in hospice volunteers who helped with nursing and gave him much-needed moral support. I was holding hands with both of them when she died.

> You overcome loneliness by becoming concerned about other people.

In time, Alan and Rhonda were able to come to the point of realizing they had done everything they could for their loved ones. It was time to let go and move on. I'll always remember the day Alan called to say he and Rhonda wanted to be married. I have never enjoyed performing a wedding more.

To release your attachment doesn't mean to forget or to deny the importance of that part of your life. It doesn't mean you do not love your deceased child or spouse or parent. It means you understand this person will not be a part of your present life, but will live only in your memories. You are ready to release your attachment so you can move on—to open new doors to a life for yourself.

Use the exercises "Writing a Letter of Good-bye" (page 198) and "Making Peace with Grief" (page 208) to help you facilitate this release.

Reorient

The next step in reaching out to a new life involves giving yourself permission to begin reorienting your interests and activities in new directions.

You will not overcome loneliness by thinking about solutions. You will not release an attachment to the past by waiting for that attachment to subside. You overcome loneliness by becoming concerned about other people. Once you discover that you are your own best friend, you can share your friendship with other people. You don't just think about it, however: You *do* it.

Those people I know who have done the most to eliminate loneliness from their lives after a major loss are the most involved in helping other bereaved people, community service, devotion to family members, and developing new friendships.

Releasing your attachment to the past is also a "doing" behavior, in which you reorient your attachments to the present. For a widow or widower, that might mean a new relationship with a person of the opposite sex. For the parent who has lost a child, it might mean focusing attention on another child in the family, having a baby, or adopting a child. In a new city, it means developing loyalties to local sports teams, joining civic groups, and getting to know the special features of that community.

The suggestions in the section "It's Okay to Live Again" (page 212) are simple but effective ways to begin opening doors to new experiences. Try them, or use the suggestions to help you think of others you could try. Another good approach is to think of something you wanted to do before your loss, but could not. Do that thing now.

Susan always wanted to go on a rafting trip through the Grand Canyon. Her husband, Jim, would have no part of it. The subject was the source of more than a few family fights. When Jim got cancer, Susan forgot all about the raft and the river. She devoted all of her energies to Jim and their remaining time together.

About fourteen months after Jim's death, Susan took their two sons on a river trip through the Grand Canyon. It was a difficult decision for her, and she had moments of tears and sadness during the trip. But it was the turning point in her grief recovery. She has now gone back to school, has a good job, and recently had her first date, much to her sons' amusement.

Richard and Janna were married for ten stormy years. They were in counseling almost from the beginning, but to no avail. Whatever else they could do in life, they could not seem to be nice to each other. They tried separating, but felt so strongly drawn to each other that they moved back together again. They fought over everything, including money, how to raise their child, and what to do on Saturday evening.

Finally, they separated again, but neither one could seem to initiate a divorce. Even living apart did not prevent them from quarreling. In time, each of them began living with another member of the opposite sex. Richard and his new girlfriend had a child, but still he could not break the emotional tie with Janna. His life was in chaos. He used drugs, drank too much alcohol, and wound up in trouble for failure to pay taxes.

It was a matter of years until Richard could work through the loss of his marriage to Janna. The day finally came when the divorce was finalized. A few months later, he and Rebecca were married.

With the ties finally broken, Richard was ready to have his life go in a new direction. He paid off his debts, quit using drugs, and no longer abused alcohol. The last I heard, he had saved for the down payment on a house.

Whatever your loss, the time comes eventually to focus on the way your life is now, rather than the way it had been before your loss, and to head in a new direction. Make a list of things you can do now that you could not do before. Make an effort to begin meeting new people. As you do, write down your feelings about the experience in your journal.

Reconnect

Reconnecting is the final step. At this point in your life, you have re-oriented your emotions to things in the present. You are able to love another person in marriage, if that is a possible alternative for you. You do not feel compelled to visit the gravesite of your child, although you may place flowers there on holidays, birthdays, and other special dates.

I remember very clearly the occasion almost three years after we moved away from our home state for the first time. From the time we moved, going back to our former state always felt like going home. Our sense of loss was so great we often shed tears as we crossed the border returning to our new state. This time, almost three years after our move, we realized that returning to our new state now felt like going home. We paused at the border and shed a few tears at the realization, but these were tears of joy.

I can't tell you when you will be ready for another marriage, another child, a different job, or a new city. Perhaps you will never choose any of those. The important thing is for you to be able to do these things, if you want to.

When you have released the past, reoriented to the future, and re-connected to the present, you will still have problems simply because you are alive, but loneliness will not be one of them.

Loss and Sexuality

If you are widowed or divorced, the issue of sex is a significant factor in your new life after loss.

I find that those who are widowed have a more difficult time talking about sexuality than those who are divorced. A part of this may be the relative ages at which people are widowed or divorced. It is not that widows in their sixties and seventies are not interested in sexual contact. They come from an era when the subject of sex was not discussed in public—and certainly not with their minister!

If you are a woman who has lost her husband to death, you are one of the ten million widows in the United States. There are about twice the number of new widows each year as widowers. Because of this, most older men are married; most older women are not.

After listening to both divorced and widowed people talk, it seems to me that those who are widowed remain celibate longer than those who are divorced. Most of that has to do with the sense of loyalty the widowed person has to his or her deceased spouse. In addition, a crazy cultural "rule" in our society says it is more appropriate for a divorced person to satisfy the desire for intimacy than a widowed person.

That seems particularly strange when you consider the widowed person has usually come from a relationship where there was more intimacy for a longer time than the divorced person.

Both widowed and divorced persons say that casual sexual encounters are a bigger problem for them than the frustration and loneliness of abstinence.

Finding ways to sublimate sexual energy is helpful for many people. Anything you do that is artistic, creative, and social will use some part of your sexuality in creative ways. A few brave people have said openly that masturbation relieves tension for a while but does nothing about the need for talking with, holding, and caressing another person.

I urge you to speak out about the problem. It needs discussion in groups and with counselors. There are no easy or pat answers. Being judgmental or moralistic with yourself or others serves no useful purpose.

In her excellent book *Beginnings: A Book for Widows*, Betty Jane Wylie speaks for widowed and divorced persons when she says, "The limits of your behavior lie within you and not in the acceptance of society around you."[1]

Money Matters

Money is part of the pathway of your recovery. It may seem like a big jump from sex to money, but both are issues of particular importance to those who are widowed or divorced.

When I asked a group of widows what they would most like to tell young couples to prepare them for the loss of a mate, they responded unanimously with concerns about money matters.

If you are widowed or divorced, your income level has probably declined. If you are a woman, you may have had to find a job for the first time in years. If you are a divorced man with children, you have learned the expensive facts of child support and keeping two residences.

Chances are, you need to know more about budgeting and the use of credit cards than you needed to before. My widowed friends would tell you to take a class in bookkeeping if your deceased spouse kept the checkbook and paid the bills. My divorced friends who are women would tell you, if you are a woman, to build your own line of credit as soon as you can. Make a small purchase you can easily afford and pay it off promptly.

Nutrition and Your New Life

Nutrition and physical fitness are vital components of your recovery. Far too little is said about the roles of food and exercise in grief recovery. The more I learn about the importance of these factors, the more I understand why some people are able to handle their grief so much better than others.

Rey came to see me because he was depressed. He was not adjusting well to career setbacks and personal disappointments. He had been to psychologists and psychiatrists. He had taken medication for depression and been in group therapy for social maladjustment. None of it was helping. He was feeling worse.

Knowing the highly skilled nature of the treatment he had already received, I didn't want to see Rey. I tried to refer him to a psychologist, but he refused. I made an appointment with him not knowing what to try next.

When Rey came in and we began to talk, something he said triggered my interest in his diet. He was a bit rattled that I wanted to talk about the things he ate instead of his emotional problems. He was more rattled when I asked him to see a local nutritionist before we talked further.

The next day he called me in an excited and hopeful voice. Testing had shown he was suffering from hypoglycemia—low blood sugar. In extreme cases it can dramatically affect moods.

That was surely the case with Rey. By changing his diet, his depression was gone in less than two weeks. His ability to relate with others returned to normal. He was able to work at adjusting to his losses with a new energy and determination. None of the former problems have recurred.

Rey could have gone through therapy for years, taken medication, and still watched his self-esteem sink steadily lower. All he needed to begin a whole new life was a change in the foods he was eating.

It is as important for you to pay attention to your nutrition through-out the length of your grief recovery as it was for Rey. You may not have a blood-sugar problem, but what you are eating or not eating can have an effect on your energy level and ability to cope with the stress of the grieving process.

Caffeine and alcohol are stimulants and will not help you handle the stress of grief. Getting all the needed nutrients from the food you eat is one of the most positive things you can do for yourself. It will be more difficult to ensure that you get all the important nutrients if your diet includes large quantities of high-fat or high-sugar foods. See Appendix A for more detailed nutrition guidelines.

> What you are eating or not eating can have an effect on your energy level and ability to cope with the stress of the grieving process.

One of the best investments in yourself you can make as you do grief work is to consult a nutritional expert. Your doctor or local hospital should be able to make a referral. Ask the nutrition expert about the right things to eat and the foods to avoid.

Physical Fitness

I also urge you to get whatever amount of physical exercise you can tolerate. Walking is one of the best exercises and a great resource for combating depression.

> Walking is one of the best exercises and a great resource for combating depression.

It's always a good idea to have a check-up by your doctor before beginning any strenuous exercise program.

Most cities have health spas or clubs. Sometimes health plans offer their members exercise classes through hospitals at a slightly dis-counted rate. If you can afford the cost, a health-club membership or exercise classes make an effective social as well as fitness contribution to your stamina for grief work.

Getting on with Life

One of the great discoveries of the journey from loss to life is that you can be your own best friend as you make your way along the pathway to grief recovery.

The exercises I have suggested provide ways you can help yourself regain a zest for living and a deep sense of happiness. It isn't easy and it doesn't come quickly. But you can emerge from the depths of your loss as one who is on top of life.

One day you will sense it is time to leave the past and get on with the present and the future. When that day comes, you will have completed the journey and finished the work. You will be a whole person again.

20

Preparing for Loss

A new dimension in wholeness

"There is no way to prepare for the loss of a loved one." You have heard this said many times—you may have said it yourself. However, regardless of how many of us may believe there is no way to prepare for loss, *it isn't true!*

You *can* prepare for losses, including the death of a spouse, child, parent, sibling or friend; divorce; moving to a new city or state; retiring from work; children leaving home; major surgery; the loss of a job; and any other major change in life.

If you have not experienced a major loss, you need to know you are not helpless before the prospect of such an inevitable event in your life. If you have experienced a major loss in the past, you need to know this doesn't guarantee you won't face other losses in the future. Even if you weren't prepared the first time, there is no reason not to be prepared now.

Marge, whose husband had been ill for many years, described her anxiety about his declining health. She said, "I feel like an ant in the path of an avalanche. Everything is out of control and rushing toward me. All I can do is wait for his death because I know it's coming. I don't talk about it because I don't know of anything I can do about it. I wait in silence."

Breaking the Silence

> The first thing you can do to prepare for loss is break the conspiracy of silence surrounding it.

The first thing you can do to prepare for loss is break the conspiracy of silence surrounding it. It's okay to talk about death. A certain superstition many people know says, "If you talk about something bad, it will happen." I think most of us realize that is a silly notion—but still we keep silent.

A widow said to me, "Bill and I never talked about death. He always believed if we talked about it, one of us would die." They didn't talk about death, but he died anyway at the age of eighty. His widow was left with many things she had never told him and a deep sense of guilt to compound the pain of her grief.

Two years after his death she could no longer keep up the many plants and trees he had planted around their home. She had meant to tell him she couldn't garden like him because of her arthritis, but never got around to it. She was afraid he would be upset because she was planning for his demise. Finally, she had the plants removed. She went through months of deep depression afterward because she was certain she had failed to meet his expectations of her.

Preparing for Loss Is Preparing for Life

Preparing for loss is not a morbid activity. It is not to become a pessimist about life, but an optimist who is also a realist. It is not to say, *Bad things will happen if I think about loss*. It is to say, *I can get through any loss in my life successfully*.

> Preparing for loss is to say, I can get through any loss in my life successfully.

By preparing for grief, you will not avoid its pain or the steps through grief described in this book. I know of no way to get under, over, or around the heartache of a major loss. Preparing for loss means strengthening yourself for the task of taking charge of your grief and working your way through it. It isn't easy or fun. But it is necessary and possible.

As soon as you decide you can do things to prepare for life's inevitable losses, you have begun to take charge of your own destiny. Taking charge in this way can be a new experience in itself, and a positive one. You will no longer feel as vulnerable or helpless as you did before. The unforeseen, unpredictable circumstances of life won't have the same power to terrify you.

I was having a day of fun with my grandchildren when the telephone interrupted me with a call from a family whose three-year-old daughter had been killed in an accident. Tragic events do happen in this world! You can't always avoid them. But you can be prepared to face the grief that follows such losses.

> I remind every couple who comes to me for premarital counseling that every marriage ends in one of two ways, death or divorce. I know of no other options. It helps to give newlyweds a realistic frame of reference for all of their planning and relating.

Preparing Your Body for Grief

Physical health is as important as mental health in working your way through a major loss. Good nutrition, physical exercise, adequate fluids, and sufficient rest are all important during mourning. They are equally important as a means of preparing for grief. Whatever your age or physical limitations might be, you can achieve an optimum level of health for you personally with surprisingly little effort.

I suggest checking with your doctor to find the best dietary plan and level of exercise for your particular situation. Don't wait until you experience a loss to take care of yourself.

Nobody Does Grief Work Perfectly

In my experience, those who have unrealistic expectations of themselves do not handle grief and loss very well. If you are a person who always demands just a little more of yourself, you will add unnecessary frustration and guilt to your grief. Nobody does grief work perfectly. It is a time of slipping and sliding, of three steps forward and two back, of doing your best and discovering there is always more to do.

Before you experience a loss is a good time to look for any unrealistic personal standards you may have and work on changing expectations of yourself. Learn to be more patient with yourself *before* you have to face the challenge of grief.

> Getting in touch with your feelings about the possibility of such events is a way of beginning to prepare for losses that are unavoidable.

Even if you have not already experienced a major loss, work through some of the exercises in this book. Ask yourself how you think you would respond to the death of a loved one, relocating to another area far from familiar sights and faces, or a divorce. Getting in touch with your feelings about the possibility of such events is a way of beginning to prepare for losses that are unavoidable.

Loss and grief are not enjoyable experiences for anyone, but they happen to all of us at some time and usually more than once. You can prepare for loss in the simple but important ways I have outlined here.

Perhaps the greatest benefit of preparing is not what preparation does for life after loss, but what it does for life *before* loss. You will live with more confidence and less fear. You will know that you have more than good luck going for you. The quality of your life will be better. Doing good things for yourself physically, mentally, and spiritually will add greater energy and enjoyment to your life.

People who successfully make their way through grief have a new-found sense of strength and self-esteem. They have faced the unimaginable and conquered it. They know that one loss does not give them immunity from other losses. But having made it through once, they also know that they can do it again, if necessary. By preparing yourself for the inevitable losses that come to all of us, you can gather some of that strength and self-esteem before any major loss confronts you.

The final thing I want you to do before you close this book is take a fantasy trip that can be a healing journey. The images it presents will seem as deep and impossible as recovering from the worst loss you can imagine. But you can follow the fantasy and make the journey. You will come out of it feeling some of the inner peace that can be yours when the pathway through grief is completed.

As you read the words that follow, allow your imagination to take you through the experience it describes.

The Secret Box

You are in a meadow. It is a beautiful, green place with wavy grass and a scattering of colorful flowers. The sky is blue overhead with just a few puffs of white clouds. (Close your eyes for a moment and create this scene in your imagination. When you are ready to go on, open your eyes and continue reading.)

You walk through the meadow and come to a crystal-blue lake. There is a short, sandy beach, so you take off your shoes and feel the grainy sand, warmed by the bright sunlight.

You walk across the beach to the water and wade in a short distance. Now you can feel the coolness of the water as compared to the warmth of the sand. It is very pleasant. (If you like, take a moment to close your eyes again and let your imagination take you into this scene. When you are ready to continue, open your eyes and read on.)

This is the amazing part. You walk farther into the water, feeling it come up around your knees, then your waist. The lake bottom is very smooth and sandy, with no rocks or weeds. You continue to walk into the cool, clear water as it rises to your chest, then your neck.

The great thing about a fantasy is that we are not limited by the usual constraints of our physical world. So, you continue walking into the water until you are under the surface! Wonder of wonders, you can breathe the water as though it were air, and you do not float. The sights around you are beautiful and you feel secure and elated. The water is cool and refreshing around you and, as you breathe it, you know why fish are so energetic. (You may want to lay down the book again for a moment and close your eyes to get the full effect. When you are ready, go on reading.)

As you walk deeper, the light grows dimmer, except for a very strong beam of sunlight that pierces the water at the very center of the lake. As you approach that place, you see a small box lying on the sand. It is shaped like a small pirate's chest, is made of dark wood, and has a brass handle.

You pick up the box and open it. The light from the sunbeam illuminates the contents so you can see them clearly. You know what is in the box. (Close your eyes so that your imagination can see it very distinctly. When you are sure you know what is there, open your eyes and continue reading.)

You close the box and carry it with you out of the water and up onto the shore. As you walk toward the meadow, a figure appears. It is a man. He walks toward you. Though he is a stranger, you are drawn to him. He smiles, and you know you have nothing to fear.

As you draw near to the stranger, you are surprised because you feel completely at ease. You say nothing, and the man says nothing. You are standing very close, and you just look into each other's eyes.

Without a word, you hold out the box, and the man reaches out and takes it. You look at each other for a minute longer, then he nods, and you turn and walk away.

You walk back through the meadow feeling the warm sun on your back and a gentle breeze around you. You walk more lightly than you have in a long time. You know inside that life is really good after all. And you are healed.

When you are finished with this story, put down the book. Stand up and walk around for a minute or two. Notice that you feel a little bit lighter than you did when you began reading.

Life after Loss

Earlier, I suggested that talking with someone who had recovered from grief was like talking to an adventurer. I said those who conquered grief talk more about what they have found than what they have lost. Their lives reflect the events of the past, but are focused on the future. Death and loss do not dominate their thoughts. They have a sense of joy that is more solid than most people's because they know there is nothing life can deal that they can't handle. They are compassionate people. They have more patience than most folks. They have a reverence for life and a deep appreciation for human relationships.

It is my hope and prayer that when you have made your way through your grief as you have through this book, others will think that talking to you is like talking to an adventurer.

May your life after loss be full and rewarding!

APPENDIX A

The Role of Nutrition in Grief Recovery

The role of nutrition in grief recovery does not get the attention it deserves. A diet complete in all the necessary nutrients is crucial to maintaining your health during the long and stressful time it takes to work through a major loss.

Maintaining an appropriate weight is the first step. We each respond to stress differently. Some people tend to eat more when stressed, and consequently gain weight, while others become disinterested in food and therefore lose weight. In either instance, if the gain or loss is more than 10 percent of your usual weight, it is likely that you will be lacking essential nutrients, and your energy to cope with stress will be decreased.

> A wide variety of foods and adequate quantities are the cornerstones of a good diet.

To help conserve energy, prepare simple meals using casseroles and one-dish meals or choose from entrées and dinners that are well-balanced but not too high in fat or salt. Use your blender, Crock-Pot, microwave, or toaster oven to save effort. Let friends or relatives help if they offer to prepare a dish or meal for you. Occasionally take advantage of a local restaurant's home-delivery service. Use whatever means works for you. Just be sure *not* to skip meals or rely on only a few foods for all your nutrition. A wide variety of foods and adequate quantities are the cornerstones of a good diet.

Fluids are also very important. Your body needs water to keep all the systems working properly and to keep essential nutrients in proper balance. Beverages that are high in caffeine or contain alcohol can act as diuretics and therefore lead to further dehydration. Just plain water is the best fluid you can take!

> Fluids are also very important.

The following guidelines are provided for your reference. They are sound, commonsense points that will assure you of a diet that will help, not hinder, your recovery, and that will be good for you for the rest of your life. If you have special dietary needs or desire more detailed nutrition information, a registered dietitian (R.D.) is best qualified to help. Your local hospital is an excellent resource.

Dietary Guidelines

1. Establish a regular schedule for meals and snacks and stick to it.

2. Drink at least eight glasses (eight ounces each) of water a day.
   Use the following food groups and quantities as a daily guide:

   - Wholegrain breads and cereals—4 to 6 servings
   - Fruits and vegetables—4 to 6 servings
   - Low-fat dairy products—2 servings
   - Meat and meat substitutes—4 to 6 ounces

3. Smaller, more frequent meals may be easier to eat than three large meals. Make sure your snacks are nutritious and that your total daily intake is still adequate.

4. Plan your meals and snacks in advance to ensure balanced, adequate meals, and to make shopping less time- and energy-consuming.

5. Eat iron-rich foods more often, including lean meats, seafood, fortified bread and cereals, leafy green vegetables, dried fruits, nuts, dried peas, and beans.

6. Carbohydrates are most easily digested by your body and are its best source of energy to help you overcome the fatigue that is often associated with grief. Include at least one serving of complex carbohydrates (not sugars) at each meal, such as bread, crackers, cereal, pasta, potatoes, rice, and dried peas and beans.

7. All the needed vitamins and minerals can be obtained from the food you eat if the recommended quantities are included daily. If your intake is not adequate or is adequate only sporadically, a supplement may be appropriate. However, large quantities of some vitamins and minerals can be harmful. Consult a registered dietitian if you feel you need supplements.

8. Once a month write down everything you eat for three days and compare your daily totals with the recommended daily amounts from each food group.

9. Weigh yourself once a week, preferably first thing in the morning. If you begin to see significant changes, talk with your physician or a registered dietitian.

Sample Menu

Breakfast
- Citrus fruit or juice
- Wholegrain toast with small amount of margarine

- Egg, egg substitute, or reduced-fat cheese
- Low-fat milk, decaffeinated coffee, or herbal tea

Lunch

- Sandwich: wholegrain bread, roll, or bagel; mustard or reduced-fat mayonnaise; lean meat, fish, or cheese; lettuce, tomato, onion, peppers, etc.
- Bean salad or coleslaw
- Fresh or canned fruit
- Decaffeinated, non-alcoholic beverage

Dinner

- Lean meat, skinless poultry, or fish: broiled, baked, or poached
- Potato with skin, brown rice, or whole-wheat pasta
- Dark green or yellow vegetable
- Fruit salad
- Low-fat pudding or yogurt
- Decaffeinated, non-alcoholic beverage

Snacks

- Pretzels or popcorn
- Wheat crackers or bagel chips
- Graham crackers or plain cookies
- Dried or fresh fruit
- Raw vegetables
- Low-fat milk, yogurt, or cheeses
- Nuts, nut butters, seeds, or granola (although these are higher in fat)

Note: Thanks to Sister Joneen Keuler, R.D., clinical dietitian at Tucson Medical Center in Tucson, Arizona, for the material in Appendix A and a review of nutrition-related comments throughout the text.

APPENDIX B

Words that Describe Feelings

It is not easy to put feelings into words. The task becomes more difficult when our feelings are very strong either positively or negatively. We commonly say, "The sunset was beautiful beyond words," or "I love you more than words can say." We also say, "There are no words to describe the pain I feel because of his death."

To be able to put our feelings into words is important even though it is difficult. Describing our feelings of grief is an act of healing.

The primary reason we have so much trouble talking about our feelings is the language we use. We commonly say "I feel" when, in fact, we are saying "I think." We say "I feel that the best way to do this is . . . " That sentence describes a thought, not a feeling. Misuse of the phrase "I feel" creates a block to expressing our feelings easily.

The simplest way to be sure you are describing feelings instead of thoughts is to test if substituting the phrase "I think" for "I feel" changes the meaning of what you are saying. If you are describing your feelings, changing the phrase will not make sense. For instance, to say, "I feel miserable and in the dumps because of my loss" makes sense, but to say, "I *think* miserable and in the dumps . . . " does not. The first sentence accurately describes your feelings.

However, if you say, "I feel my experience of loss is the worst thing to happen to me," you can change the statement to "I *think* my experience of loss is the worst thing to happen to me" and still make sense. In this case you would not be describing your feelings, but instead, a thought you have about your loss.

> Describing our feelings of grief is an act of healing.

The following words describe feelings. As you write in your journal or work through the various exercises in the book, refer to this list often. Find the best word to describe the feeling you are trying to describe.

Happy

content	merry
relaxed	exhilarated
serene	elated
peaceful	jubilant
joyous	carefree
glad	lighthearted
cheerful	ecstatic

Angry

outraged	seething
irritated	infuriated
furious	enraged
cross	bitter
annoyed	fuming
tantrum	wrathful
burning	frustrated

Sad

sour	discouraged
miserable	depressed
bleak in	the dumps
unhappy	flat
dismal	melancholy
dreary	forlorn
mournful	joyless

Fearful

shaky	anxious
panicky	scared
hysterical	petrified
shocked	alarmed
horrified	

Tense

taut	paralyzed
uptight	stretched
tense	hollow
weak	breathless
immobilized	

Hurt

injured	pained
offended	suffering
afflicted	lonely
aching	distressed
crushed	cold
tortured	

Courageous

encouraged	brave
confident	determined
secure	proud
reassured	daring
bold	

Eager

fascinated	avid
creative	sincere
earnest	intrigued
excited	inquisitive
keen	

Doubtful

unbelieving	powerless
suspicious	hesitant
uncertain	defeated
wavering	pessimistic
hopeless	

Tired

heavy	subdued
fatigued	worn out
exhausted	burnt out
weary	spent
lethargic	

APPENDIX C

Forming a Support Group

Forming a grief support group is fairly easy to do. Because major loss is such a universal human experience, you will have little difficulty finding people in your community who are willing to participate.

One of your first tasks will be to decide what the focus of the group will be. Will it be just for widows and widowers? Or, will it also include those who have lost children, parents, or other loved ones? Will it focus only on the grief that follows death? Do you want to address the needs of divorced persons? Do you want the group limited to people in your church or neighborhood?

If you are going to be the one to form the group, reflect on your own situation and needs and start from there.

Be assured that once you have penetrated people's initial anxiety about meeting with strangers, you will find a positive response.

Churches, synagogues, clubs, fraternal organizations, PTA groups, and your own circle of friends are all good places to seek participants for a support group.

You can call a group together in several ways. The following have all been used successfully:

1. Ask your minister, priest, or rabbi to publish a notice in their newsletter about the formation of a support group. Ask people to submit their names. Include your name and telephone number for additional information.
2. Put a notice in a club or fraternal group's newsletter. Offer to let the group meet at your home or arrange for another place.
3. Consult a local psychologist about offering a six- to eight-session series on grief and loss. Often, a counselor or psychologist will do it free of charge for potential referrals.
4. Talk to friends about getting together to support each other in times of loss and to share past experiences.
5. Publish a notice in your local newspaper or post flyers in markets, drugstores, and other public-display places announcing the formation of the group.

Whatever approach you take, be specific about the group's purpose, length of time it will meet, and cost, if any.

It is always good to put an end date on the initial series of meetings. This encourages people to be regular in attendance and provides a "safety valve" in case anyone has emotional problems that are too severe for the group to handle.

Have each participant get a copy of this book to use as a guide.

Groups should consist of at least four people, but no more than ten without a trained leader.

Unless a professional counselor is called in, it is important that whoever calls the group together leads the first series of meetings.

If the group is not lead by a trained professional, its purpose will be different. *Untrained persons should not attempt therapy with members of the group.* However, providing a setting where people can freely share experiences and feelings and find a network of others who care is extremely helpful. A self-help format requires only that the leader understand the principles of grief recovery explained in this book.

The fundamental principles for a self-directed group are these:

- Feelings are neither right nor wrong. The leader must be as accepting of anger and frustration as of hopefulness and joy.
- It takes a long time to work through loss and grief.
- Review the steps of grief recovery in Chapter 5.

Session One: Telling Our Story

The first session is especially important. People often feel uncomfortable and anxious about what is going to take place. It is important for the leader to establish an atmosphere of relaxed security. If a professional counselor is not present, there are several ways to do this:

- Provide a comfortable, "homey" setting. Soft lights (not dim), comfortable chairs arranged in a circle, easy-to-read name tags, and isolation from other distracting noises all help to establish the kind of setting that is needed.
- Children should not be present because they are too distracting. Childcare may have to be provided at a different location.
- Refreshments, if any, should be restricted to light beverages until the session is completed. Alcoholic beverages can be a problem. Avoid them.
- At least one full box of tissues should be within easy reach at every session. (I keep five full boxes on hand and deliberately set one out on a table or empty chair as each session begins.)

Begin by reminding everyone of the group's purpose. Have each person give his or her name and tell why he or she is coming to the group. Everyone should describe the loss they have experienced in as much detail as they wish. Encourage them to use the names of deceased or divorced persons.

It is important at this point of the group's life together that others just listen and not give advice. It is common to hear repeatedly, "I thought I was the only one who felt like that." It helps if the leader calls attention to the common ground of the group's experiences.

The main goal of the meeting is for people to tell their stories and to know they have been listened to and understood.

The group should meet for no more than ninety minutes and should end on time. Using prayer at the closing is a matter of personal choice. If prayer is used, it should be short, affirming, and not "preachy."

It is good to create a roster of the group and have a printed list of names, addresses, and telephone numbers ready for each participant at the second meeting.

Session Two: Four Key Facts about Grief

The setting should be prepared again as it was for the first meeting.

- Be sure the box of tissues is clearly visible and easily reachable.
- Use name tags again if group members do not already know each other or if new persons are joining.

Have each member of the original group introduce himself to the newcomers and briefly tell his losses. Then the new people are welcomed to share their stories.

Present the "Four Key Facts about Grief" as described in Chapter 7. Take time for group discussion on each one and how various members are experiencing it. Don't rush. You may take up the entire evening with just the first one: *The way out of grief is through it, because there is no way around it.*

It is quite possible that tears will flow during the discussion. Always affirm to the group the appropriateness of crying.

If time remains, ask people to describe the particular problems they have faced in the past week. Keep in mind that where people are in their grief process will determine the focus of their sharing.

In closing, ask people to identify themselves if they are willing to be called at home by others in the group. Urge group members to put a mark by these names on their rosters. The support that group members sometimes give each other in these informal, between-sessions contacts is often as helpful as the meetings themselves. It is not unusual to see lasting friendships develop in this way.

Session Three: Moods and Feelings

Begin the session by asking if anyone has anything to share with the group. There maybe a tendency to sidetrack onto issues not directly related to the individual's grief recovery. For instance, if someone is in the stage of blaming others for the loss, that person may take up excessive time talking about those others instead of his or her own feelings. If this occurs, it is the task of the leader to bring the focus of conversation back to the immediate experience of the group members. Do it gently.

Pass out paper and pencils. Have the group diagram their moods over the past year according to the instructions beginning on page 86. Ask them to describe their feelings at the moment in terms of a color, taste, smell, touch, and sound.

Have each person write an answer to this question: If I could change one thing in my life right now, what would it be?

Give everyone adequate time to do all of the above assignments. When the answers have been recorded, go around the group and discuss one question at a time. Try to draw out feelings and more detailed descriptions if anyone gives only superficial, brief responses.

Before closing, give each person the following "homework" assignment:

- Purchase a stenographer's notepad and label it *Journal.*
- Record each day for the next week:
    a significant event that happened;
    the person who was most important to me today;
    feelings of which I was most aware today;
    plans for tomorrow.
- Note date and time of day of entries at top of page.
- Bring journal to the group next week.

Session Four: Keeping a Journal

Begin this and all subsequent sessions with the same invitation to share that was given in Session Three.

Ask for sharing about people's experience with keeping a journal. It is common for some group members to have either "forgotten" (repressed) the assignment or completed only part of it. Be sure to acknowledge that this is okay and they can try again.

Ask those who are willing to share some portion of their journal entries. You may want to ask them to choose a particular day and share the entries from that day.

Ask the group members to continue keeping a journal for the rest of the group sessions. They should add the following notations:

- Changes I observe happening to me
- Notes to myself

As the group moves into more personal sharing, it is natural for some people to report feeling worse at the end of the meeting than they did when they arrived. *Assure participants that this is normal* and a significant sign of growth. It is not a sign of slipping backward, but of moving forward. It is not a negative occurrence, but a necessary, positive one, even though it is uncomfortable. It will pass, and they will feel much better if they stay with the process.

If people drop out at this time, try to maintain contact and help them establish some other support base.

If any group member seems to manifest the symptoms of distorted grief as described on pages 59 and 60, encourage that person to seek the help of a professional counselor or psychologist.

Close the session in whatever way has become appropriate and effective for your group.

Session Five: Growing through Loss

After any open sharing, review the following guidelines for growing through loss which are described in some detail in Chapter 8:

- Believe that your grief has a purpose and an end.
- Be responsible for your own grief process.
- Don't be afraid to ask for help.
- Don't rush it.

Discuss how group members are experiencing each of these guidelines. In which areas are they having the most problems? In which areas do they seem to have a good grasp on their grief?

To close, lead the group in doing the 8–8–8 Breather exercise beginning on page 183. Repeat the sequence several times. When finished with the exercise, join hands in a circle and give each other words of encouragement for the next week.

Session Six: The Influence of Religion on Grief

After giving an opportunity for open sharing, ask the group to talk about the positive and negative ways religious faith has affected their grief experience.

It is especially important, when dealing with the subject of religion, that people's individual views and feelings are recognized. Some people are very angry at God. Some cannot express that anger; some will deny it altogether. Others may have abandoned their faith as a result of their grief. Still others will look to their faith as the foundation for trying to put life back together again. You may find people who are convinced that God is punishing them. Others may tell you that God has taken their loved one. Whatever a person's feelings might be, the most helpful thing the group can do is just listen.

Avoid getting into philosophical discussions about the presence of evil in the world, why tragic things happen to good people, or whether God punishes people through grief experiences.

Ask group members to keep their sharing personal and to accept the sharing of others, even if it is quite different from their own experience.

At the close of the session, do the 8–8–8 Breather exercise (page 183). Repeat the sequence several times. If the group is open to it, close the meeting by joining hands in a circle and offering a short prayer of gratitude. I ask directly, "Would you be comfortable if we had a prayer before we close?" I find that people will give an honest answer if an open and accepting atmosphere has been established during the session. If some wish to have prayer and others do not, allow those who do not to exercise the option of excluding themselves. The prayer should be brief, positive, and hopeful.

Remind everyone to keep writing in their journals on a daily basis. You may want to review the instructions from Session Three.

Session Seven: Coping with Forgetfulness

Begin by asking participants to share something significant from their journal writing of the past week. After all have had an opportunity to share, ask if anyone is having problems with forgetfulness.

You can be sure that many are experiencing this.

Locking keys in the car; misplacing house keys; and forgetting appointments, telephone numbers, and people's names are common after a major loss. Assure the group that such behavior is a normal part of the grief experience for many people.

Encourage people to keep an extra set of car keys in a magnetic box somewhere under a fender or have an extra door key kept separately from the rest of their keys. It's a good idea to have a trusted neighbor keep a set of house keys. Even the most familiar and frequently used telephone numbers and addresses should be written down and kept in a visible place.

Ask these additional questions:

- Has anyone here wondered if you are the only one having these kinds of problems with grief?

- Do you find that routine tasks have become more difficult to do?
- Do you ever wonder if you are going crazy?

You will find that most people in the group have experienced all or some of these symptoms of grief. It's called *fragmenting,* and it's totally normal in the first three to six months after a major loss. Those who have moved beyond this stage will remember when it happened to them. I have talked with people whose loss was more than five years old and they had never told anyone about the fragmenting symptoms. Just talking about them and discovering that other people experience similar symptoms often helps lift a heavy weight from the shoulders of bereaved people.

One of the beneficial "spin-offs" of this sharing is the common bond it can create among those who are divorced and those who are widowed. Often, if widowed and divorced persons are in the same group, a certain amount of tension exists among them. Exercises such as this one help relieve that tension by focusing on reactions to loss and grief that are common to both.

If time permits after the discussion on forgetfulness, ask the group to talk about any problems they are having with nongrieving people. This is another subject that brings grieving people closer to each other.

Have the group review the section in Chapter 17 that addresses the subject of relating to nongrievers, pages 191 to 193.

As a homework assignment for the next week, ask the group to focus on forgiveness in their journal writing.

- Whom do you need to forgive for failing to respond to your loss in a helpful way?
- Do you blame anyone for your loss?
- Do you need to forgive yourself for anything?

Sharing on this forgiveness will open the next session of the group.

Close by joining hands in a circle and having members of the group give expressions of the unity they feel with the others as a result of their experiences together over the past six weeks.

Session Eight: Sleep Issues

Open the session by asking the group to share on the forgiveness issues they focused on in their journals during the past week.

Next, ask the group to respond to these questions:

- Who has been a significant person in my life this week?
- What did this person do for me?

After this sharing is completed, ask if anyone in the group ever has problems going to sleep or getting up. (By this time in the life of your group, the subject of sleep problems may have already come up.)

Have people share their experiences. You may find wide variations between people. Some have no problems with either sleep or feeling fatigued. Others will have problems with both of these symptoms. Again, there is great value for the participants in hearing other people's experience.

This is a good time to review the information on nutrition in Appendix A. Many times, what a person eats and drinks will result in more energy during the day and better rest at night.

Tell the group the following story about Hazel:

Hazel could not sleep after her divorce and subsequent surgery for a leg injury suffered in a fall. She was growing increasingly irritable, performing poorly at work, and gaining weight. Her leg was not healing. She went for counseling to find out what was wrong with her emotionally and spiritually. After a few minutes of gathering information, the counselor asked her to describe what she did during the evening and what food and drink she consumed after dinner—which she normally ate at about 6:00 P.M.

Hazel reported that she grew increasingly anxious as the evening went on. At first she felt a vague nervousness, but after her failure to fall asleep on a couple of occasions, she focused her anxiety on that.

To relieve the discomfort and to occupy her mind with other things, she would begin working crossword puzzles at about 9:00 P.M. She drank hot chocolate and ate cookies while working on the puzzles.

Without realizing what she was doing, Hazel was stimulating her body with sugar and caffeine while she stimulated the analytical portion of her mind with the crossword puzzles. There was no way she was going to be able to fall asleep within hours of that kind of activity and food intake.

The counselor suggested she change the hot chocolate to decaffeinated herbal tea and the cookies to raw vegetables or a dish of oatmeal with warm milk. He also suggested she substitute a book of poetry or photographic artwork for her crossword puzzles.

Within three nights, Hazel had returned to her normal sleep patterns. She also visited a local nutrition counselor for guidance on possible vitamin supplements. Only a short time later, her leg began to heal.

Focus the balance of sharing on people's response to the story of Hazel and what it says about their own experience.

As a homework assignment, have each person prepare a daily calendar for themselves for the next week. The daytime hours should be divided into three sections: morning, afternoon, and evening. Have group members list what they plan to do during each of these periods of time for the next day.

The calendar for nighttime hours after their normal bedtime should be listed in half-hour intervals. They should list what they will do during each half-hour of the night until their regular time of rising, should they wake up in the middle of the night or not be able to go to sleep.

I suggest listing tasks that the person does not like to do and usually puts off as long as possible.

This schedule should be filled out each day and followed as closely as possible. Announce that the opening sharing for Session Nine will be focused on each person's experiences with the calendar for the week.

Close the group in whatever way has become most comfortable for the participants.

Session Nine: Grief Statements

The first order of business for the session is to have everyone report on their experience with the daily calendars. Take enough time for each person to share his or her successes and failures. Assure them that whatever happened, it was okay and they can continue to use the exercise for as long as they wish.

Pass out a clean sheet of lined notebook paper to each person. Dictate the following statement. Ask each person to write it down as you read:

The sadness I feel is a badge of honor. I wear the brokenness of my life at this moment with pride.

These expressions of my grief testify to the importance of _____ (each person will fill in the name of person, place, or condition that has been lost) to me.

I am willing to feel the full impact of my grief as a final act of tribute and love. I will make my way through this experience and will not run from it.

Signed,

(Your name)

Before anyone signs the statement, take time to talk about how each one feels about it. In what way does each one see his or her grief as a badge of honor? What feelings do people have about signing this statement?

Some members of the group may want to make a change in the statement before signing it. Allow anyone to make whatever changes are necessary to make the statement true for them.

Have each person sign the statement. Then, using tape, post it on a wall where all can see it. Do this one person at a time. As each one posts his or her statement, have them read it aloud, including any changes they have made.

After all statements are posted, take time to talk about the experience.

The homework assignment for the following week is to write letters to and from one's grief. You will find a full description of this exercise on pages 96 to 98.

Close the group by having everyone gather their statements from the wall, put them in a pile on a chair, and gather around it, holding hands. Join in a short prayer or some other affirmation of what the statements represent.

Session Ten: Letter to and from Grief

Begin the session with an opportunity for open sharing about significant events of the week.

Ask people to report on their experience with writing to and from their grief. Those who have brought their letters with them may want to read them to the group.

It is important to affirm anyone who was unable to carry out the assignment. It is not unusual to have several who can't face the task at the present time. If you are accepting of everyone's experience, a valuable discussion can follow, regardless of whether the letters were written.

Talk about how people felt as they wrote each letter or found they could not write one or both of them.

When all have shared, have the group lay aside everything they are holding. Tell them the next exercise is one of relaxation as reward for all their hard work.

Everyone should get in a comfortable position with feet flat on the floor, arms and hands in laps, and eyes closed. Begin with a few repetitions of the 8–8–8 Breather exercise (page 183).

Read aloud the exercise beginning on page 208 titled "Making Peace with Grief." Your vocal tone should be peaceful and soft, but easy to hear. If you are uncomfortable reading the monologue, have someone else record it on a cassette and play it for the group.

When the exercise is completed, take time to talk about individual experiences with it. Remember, no particular response is "right." Whatever reaction people have is valid for them and will reflect their own personality and stage of grief.

As a homework assignment, ask the group to keep a daily log of their food intake, using the guidelines in Appendix A. These logs should be brought to Session Eleven.

Close the session in whatever manner has become most appropriate for your group.

Session Eleven: Grief Work and Good Nutrition

As you open this session, remind the group that you have only one more session to go. Ask people to talk about the issues of grief and loss that are most important to them at this time. What is there that each person wants the group to hear before it is disbanded? Remember, as leader, you should be ready to deal with issues of loss during this next-to-last group session. These issues, too, should be talked about freely.

Call the group's attention to the material found in Appendix A about the role of nutrition in grief recovery. Ask each person to discuss his or her daily log of food intake for the past week. Did everyone keep the log? If not, why not? If it was kept, what was learned from it about each one's nutritional strengths and weaknesses?

If it is possible to get a nutritionist to come to the meeting for this portion of it, that is a real plus.

Next, talk about what each person is doing in the area of physical fitness. Just forty-five minutes of brisk walking can do wonders for lifting spirits and easing depression. Urge everyone to have a physical examination if they haven't had one since their loss. This is especially important for those who are four to six months past a major loss experience.

Any program of exercise and fitness should be done with the involvement and direction of each person's doctor.

Close the session in the manner that is most appropriate for your group.

Session Twelve: Best Friend–Worst Enemy; The Secret Box

Plan to have some special refreshments at the close of this final session. Allow time for casual interaction and fellowship before people leave.

Open the session by reminding everyone that it is the last session. Ask for sharing about what people have gained from the sessions and how they feel about its ending.

In most cases, some of the group members will want to go on meeting. You should decide before this session whether you wish to continue in the group or as its leader. In any event, it is best to take a break of at least one week before going on.

Another decision that often must be made at this time is whether to take in new members to the group. Keep in mind that newcomers will not have gone through the exercises and experiences of the "veteran" group members. In most cases, unless a trained leader is in charge, I think it is best either to disband and start over again or to create a second group for newcomers and go on with those of the original group who wish to continue meeting.

It is very important that no one in the current group is pressured into continuing.

After everyone has shared on the opening subject, ask the group to do the exercise on page 215 titled "Best Friend–Worst Enemy." Share the results of the exercise with each other.

Close the session and the series by doing the exercise beginning on page 229 titled "The Secret Box." Narrate it rather than having the group read it individually.

When the exercise is completed, gather the group in a circle and express thanks to each other for everyone's support and caring. Close with a short prayer or other affirmative statement.

FURTHER READING

Buscaglia, Leo. *The Fall of Freddie the Leaf*. Thorofare, N.J.: Charles B. Slack Inc., 1982.

Cain, Albert. *Survivors of Suicide*. Springfield, Ill.: C. C. Thomas, 1972.

Clinebell, Howard. *Growth Counseling for Mid-Years Couples*. Minneapolis, Minn.: Fortress Press, 1977.

Colgrove, Melba, Harold Bloomfield, and Peter McWilliams. *How to Survive the Loss of a Love*. New York: Bantam, 1981.

Davidson, Glen W. *Understanding Mourning*. Minneapolis, Minn.: Augsburg, 1984.

Diamond, Harvey, and Marilyn Diamond. *Fit for Life*. New York: Warner Books, 1985.

Donnelley, Nina H. *I Never Know What to Say: How to Help Your Family and Friends Cope with Tragedy*. New York: Ballantine, 1987.

Fox, Arnold, and Barry Fox. *Immune for Life*. Rocklin, Calif.: Prima Publishing, 1990.

Gaffney, Donna. *The Seasons of Grief*. New York: NAL Books, 1988.

Ginsburg, Genevieve. *To Live Again*. New York: Jeremy P. Tarcher, Inc., 1987.

Greteman, Jim. *Coping with Divorce: From Grief to Healing*. Notre Dame, Ind.: Ave Maria Press, 1981.

Grollman, Earl. *Explaining Death to Children*. Boston: Beacon Press, 1967.

_____. *Living When a Loved One Has Died*. Boston: Beacon Press, 1977.

_____. *Talking about Death*. Boston: Beacon Press, 1990.

_____. *What Helped Me When My Loved Ones Died*. Boston: Beacon Press, 1982.

_____. *Time Remembered*. Boston: Beacon Press, 1987.

Hausman, Patricia, and Judith Berm Hurley. *The Healing Foods*. New York: Dell Publishing, 1989.

Jackson, Edgar. *The Many Faces of Grief*. Nashville: Abingdon, 1972.

_____. *Understanding Grief*. Nashville: Abingdon, 1957.

Krantzler, Mel. *Creative Divorce*. New York: Signet Books, 1974.

Kübler-Ross, Elisabeth. *On Death and Dying*. New York: MacMillan, 1969.

_____. *Living with Death and Dying*. New York: MacMillan, 1982.

_____. *Questions and Answers on Death and Dying*. New York: MacMillan, 1974.

_____. *On Children and Death*. New York: MacMillan, 1985.

Kushner, Harold S. *When Bad Things Happen to Good People*. New York: Schocken Books, 1981.

Lewis, C. S. *A Grief Observed*. New York: Bantam, 1976.

Lindemann, Erich. *Beyond Grief: Studies in Crisis Intervention*. Northvale, N.J.: Jason Aronson, Inc., 1979.

Lord, Janice Harris. *Beyond Sympathy*. Ventura, Calif.: Pathfinder Publishing, 1988.

Lynch, James. *The Broken Heart: The Medical Consequences of Loneliness*. New York: Basic Books, 1977.

Manning, Doug. *Comforting Those Who Grieve*. New York: Harper & Row, 1985.

_____. *Don't Take My Grief Away: What to Do When You Lose a Loved One*. New York: Harper & Row, 1984.

Marshall, Fiona. *Losing a Parent*. Tucson, Ariz.: Fisher Books, 1993.

Mitchell, Kenneth, and Herbert Anderson. *All Our Losses, All Our Griefs: Resources for Pastoral Care*. Louisville, Ky.: Westminster Press, 1983.

Nouwen, Henri. *A Letter of Consolation*. New York: Harper & Row, 1982.

O'Connor, Nancy. *Letting Go with Love: The Grieving Process*. Tucson, Ariz.: La Mariposa Press, 1984.

Phipps, William. *Death: Confronting the Reality*. Atlanta, Ga.: John Knox Press, 1987.

Price, Eugenia. *Getting Through the Night: Finding Your Way After the Loss of a Loved One*. New York: Walker & Co., 1985.

Sanford, Doris, and Graci Evans. *It Must Hurt a Lot*. Sisters, Oreg.: Multnomah Press, 1986.

Schiff, Harriett. *Living Through Mourning*. New York: Viking, 1986.

Shuchter, Stephen. *Dimensions of Grief*. San Francisco: Jossey-Bass Publishers, 1986.

Smoke, Jim. *Growing Through Divorce*. Irvine, Calif.: Harvest House Publishers, 1986.

_____. *Suddenly Single*. Old Tappan, N.J.: Revell, 1982.

Spiegel, Yorick. *The Grief Process: Analysis and Counseling*. Nashville: Abingdon, 1977.

Stearns, Ann Kaiser. *Living Through Personal Crisis*. Chicago: Thomas More Press, 1984.

Sullender, R. Scott. *Grief and Growth*. New York: Paulist Press, 1985.

Thielicke, Helmut. *Living with Death*. Grand Rapids, Mich.: Eerdmans, 1983.

Viorst, Judith. *Necessary Losses*. New York: Simon & Schuster, 1986.

Westburg, Granger. *Good Grief*. Minneapolis, Minn.: Fortress Press, 1962.

Wylie, Betty Jane. *Beginnings: A Book for Widows*. Toronto: McClelland and Stewart, 1997.

NOTES

Introduction

1. Viktor Frankl, *Man's Search for Meaning* (New York: Washington Square Press, Simon & Schuster, 1963).

Chapter 7

1. Glen W. Davidson, *Understanding Mourning* (Minneapolis, Minn.: Augsburg, 1984), pp. 24–27.

Chapter 11

1. Ann Kaiser Stearns, *Living through Personal Crisis* (Notre Dame, Ind.: Thomas More Publishing, 1983)

Chapter 18

1. Earl Grollman, *Time Remembered* (Boston: Beacon Press, 1987).

Chapter 19

1. Betty Jane Wylie, *Beginnings: A Book for Widows* (Toronto: McClelland and Stewart, 1997).

ACKNOWLEDGMENTS

This fourth edition of *Life after Loss* reflects experiences and insights gained over the course of twenty-five years. The list of those to whom I am indebted continues to grow.

First and foremost are the thousands of people who have shared their loss experiences with me in grief support groups, seminars, and conferences. There are all those who have found courage, guidance, and comfort from the previous editions of the book—and gave it their endorsement by recommending it to others. Some have credited the book for saving their lives.

I will forever be grateful to my mentors in the field of loss and grief. They include Dr. Earl Grollman, Dr. Glen Davidson, and Dr. Howard Clinebell Jr. These men are pioneers in grief recovery who provided the foundation upon which I could formulate the exercises and guidelines that have helped so many.

My brother, Frank Deits, continues to share his expertise with computers, as he has since the first edition was written. His wife, Mary, a professional counselor, provided valuable insights into the relationship between the body and emotions. My sister, Marilyn Witt, allowed me inside her thoughts and feelings during major losses in her life. Her vivid descriptions of the healing process are reflected throughout this edition.

I am also grateful to the people of Velda Rose United Methodist Church in Mesa, Arizona, where I served as senior minister for thirteen years. They were a living encyclopedia of wisdom and compassion as they showed me how a congregation can support people in times of loss.

I owe the most gratitude to my wife, June. She has shared my walk of life for more than fifty years. June is one of the most courageous people I have ever known—and one of the most compassionate. Her response to devastating losses in her own life has been to bring hope and comfort to others. She has read every page of every edition of *Life after Loss*. Her influence permeates this fourth edition. There would be no book without her.

—*Bob Deits*

INDEX